A MODERN DA
OF ADDICTION

FIND YOUR TRUTH

LOU REDMOND

Foreword by Alasdair Plambeck

Find Your Truth: A Modern Day Story About Letting Go of Addiction and Finding Life's Purpose

Copyright © 2017 by Lou Redmond.

All rights reserved. No part of this publication may be reproduced, distributed or transmitted in any form or by any means, including photocopying, recording, or other electronic or mechanical methods, without the prior written permission of the publisher, except in the case of brief quotations embodied in critical reviews and certain other noncommercial uses permitted by copyright law. For permission requests, write to the publisher, addressed "Attention: Permissions Coordinator," at the address below.

Lou Redmond

LouRedmond.com/contact-me

Editor: Bonnie Bertano
Cover Design: Miladinka Milic

First Edition

Find Your Truth by Lou Redmond
ISBN 978-0998577807

This book would not have been possible without the dedication from my editor and teamate, Bonnie Bertano. Bonnie, I am so grateful we met and have been brought together for this project. Thank you for putting up with hundreds of emails, last minute edits, and all my unknown throughout this process. You have been a blessing for me and deserve your Truth to shine brightly in the world. A wholehearted Thank You for your work in making this dream come true. We had fun and got it done.

Special thank you to those who backed Find Your Truth's crowdfunding campaign and gave it the extra resources to come to life. Your early support and belief was above and beyond what I could have imagined. I am so grateful for you.

To my Mom and Dad, thank you for your unconditional love and understanding. I wouldn't have been able to do this without you.

And to those who stood by me throughout my journey, thank you. Your love and support made this possible.

Dedicated to Kelly, my Angel.

We are all led to the truth for which we are ready.

— Neale Donald Walsch

FOREWORD

"Man is born free and everywhere he is in chains." - Jean-Jacques Rousseau

I met Lou in 2014 at one of the weekly Friday mastermind meetings he describes in this book. Through those weekly meetings we developed a fast friendship that carried on outside the boardroom and led to us running our first triathlon together. We have remained close friends ever since.

When I first met Lou, he was timid, quiet and seemed unsure of himself. It is only now that I can see what a pivotal moment in his life we had met at. Back then he was just beginning to take hold of the helm, but the stormy seas of self discovery still lay ahead. He was still lost and sailing on rough, open waters with no shore in sight.

I don't know that Lou anymore. The Lou I know now beams with the radiance of someone who has turned to face his own shadow and discovered an inner light beyond. Now he's shining that light on the rocks that so nearly had him shipwrecked, to help guide others still at sea toward calmer waters.

It wasn't until reading Find Your Truth that I began to understand what the hell had happened over the last couple years to have sparked such an utter transformation. Had you received a once weekly update into Lou's life during that time (as I had) you'd be excused for wondering at times if he'd lost his mind.

But it was the exact opposite. "I've really gone so sane, they think I'm insane" Lou writes, reflecting on a hilarious encounter when six policemen turn up on his doorstep uninvited after his impromptu job resignation letter was misinterpreted by coworkers as a suicide note.

Call it courage, faith, intuition or more likely all three —it's no small credit to Kelly for standing unwaveringly by Lou's side from the beginning.

Lou's story is intense, raw and real. My hands sweated and my heart raced as I retraced his tumultuous voyage through the dark troughs of mindless drug addiction and the swirling eddies of emotional turmoil it spawned, to the lofty and solitary peaks of personal revelation: he holds absolutely nothing back. It's a modern day story of recognizing the shadows on the wall, throwing off the shackles of self-bondage and walking out of the cave and into the light. And he wants to show how you can do the same.

While our stories may be different, we can all find parts of ourselves in Lou's story. Suffering is one of the basic elements of human experience that we all share —it connects and unifies us. We are all in this together. In our own ways, we all must face the precarious situation of only being "a head nod and ten dollars away from the thrill of the pill" that Lou so jarringly describes.

What you have in your hands is a brave and incredibly intimate story of self-transformation. Lou has taken great pains in these pages to share a practical set of lessons distilled from his experience that anyone can apply to spark positive change in their own life. And through sharing his own story Lou leaves us with one last lesson: that we all have our own unique story worth sharing.

There is a meditation practice in Buddhist teachings called Tong-len in which one is instructed to breathe in one's own suffering or the suffering of others and breathe out love and compassion to all those still suffering. It is from reflecting on our suffering, says the Dalai Lama, that we "develop greater resolve to put an end to the causes of suffering and the unwholesome actions and deeds which lead to suffering" and that we "increase [our] enthusiasm for engaging in the wholesome actions and deeds which lead to happiness and joy."

As I read Find Your Truth I couldn't help but see this as Lou's own version of the practice of Tong-len.

He's taken a deep breath in.

But his out breath is even greater.

-Alasdair Plambeck
Writer at AlasdairPlambeck.com

PREFACE

It was 9:00 AM and I had just finished writing an email to my entire company from home, announcing I was quitting. No two week notice, no discussions, no explanations...and it had to be effective immediately, right NOW. I poured my heart and soul into the email, thanking everyone for my time there. I clicked send then put my phone on airplane mode so I could revel in this feeling, uninterrupted.

My journal entry for today read simply: *REMEMBER, THE WAY YOU FEEL RIGHT NOW IS WORTH IT. NO MATTER HOW HARD IT GETS, HOW MANY ROADBLOCKS YOU EN-COUNTER, HOW MANY PEOPLE DOUBT YOU. I'M SORRY I EVER DID. I LOVE YOU. THANK YOU. LIFE STARTS, <u>NOW</u>.*

Later that day I sat on a bench outside of my apartment and continued writing in my journal, high on the intense emotions. I wrote about life finally making sense. I felt strongly that everything I had done in my life up to this point had led me here, to this very spot, right now. I knew I had made the right decision. If you've ever had this experience of knowing everything that happens is in some kind of divine order and you are part of it, you understand what I was feeling.

Just as I was writing about the gratitude I felt for the people in my life who had helped me get to this point, I looked to my left and saw a suburban police vehicle parked on the street. I sensed it had something to do with me.

Find Your Truth

A few minutes later, five officers walked through my gate, one of them asking: "Are you the one who's writing emails, talking about some higher calling?" A resounding *HOLY SHIT!* sounded inside my head. I responded, telling them I had just quit my job today, and asked if there was something wrong. Another one of the officers replied: "Well, people have concerns that your email might have been a suicide note."

I couldn't believe it. Here I was, never happier or more excited about life, and people thought I wanted to kill myself? When the police then asked for my ID, they didn't allow me to go inside to get it because "there could be weapons in there." I guess they didn't understand, just like someone who read my email didn't understand... that I had come to the realization that there was more to life than working eight hours a day for someone else's dream.

I assured the officers that I'd never felt better and that there was nothing to worry about. I also told them they had no right to enter my property because I hadn't done anything wrong. They seemed to be satisfied with my comments, and they left.

I realized it was time for me to get on the phone and tell people I was okay, and to try to explain what was going on with me. The problem was, how the hell could I explain that I quit a job with a company I liked, right after getting a promotion? How could I justify a decision like that when I had no plans for how I was going to make money and provide for myself?

My drastic decision didn't seem rational, and that's precisely why I'm writing this book. Some things in life just don't make sense from a logical standpoint and can't be explained, so my goal is to share the events in my life that led up to this day; the day I took a leap of faith into the unknown. My journey had actually started months before; it was a remarkable

Preface

adventure of personal growth. The changes I made and my decision that day led me to a life with purpose and meaning, joy and fulfillment.

It's my hope to inspire others with this story and introduce people to the idea that they too can make positive changes that lead to a more fulfilling life. I promise without a doubt that if an out-of-control college fratboy like me can change his life for the better, anyone can.

I appreciate you taking the time to read my story. From the bottom of my heart, I share the steps I took in my life to be able to take this leap of faith. I did something that seemed drastic, without any solid plans for the future. I experienced the uncertainty that comes with stepping into the unknown. I had no idea what I was going to do next, no idea where it would lead. All I had was the faith that came with full force: a belief, even a knowing... that I was finally on my path to true happiness.

It was a wild ride, and I hope you enjoy my story.

With Love...

Lou
San Diego, February 6th, 2015

INTRODUCTION

Truth

noun

1. That which is in accordance with fact or reality.
2. A fact or belief that is perceived as real.

If people can argue about something, then there can't be just one truth, can there? How can truth be defined when our realities are all shaped by different perspectives? What is true to one person may not be true to another, and vice versa. While I do believe in universal truth, I have to question what makes it universal. What I've learned is it's something that just can't be put into words. When you hear the truth, whether it be *your* truth or *the* truth, it's a visceral feeling and only you can tell when it resonates.

In my journey to my own truth, I had to face my fears and overcome many obstacles. I let go of habits and mindsets that no longer served me. I confronted my personal demons head-on and found my way past them or through them, not around. It's a tough thing to do and not something most people want to hear about, much less do. It's like the classic phrase from Jack Nicholson in the movie *A Few Good Men:* "You can't handle the truth!" Sometimes we can't. Sometimes we're just not ready for the truth, and that's okay.

Ultimately, the truth will come to us when we *are* ready, exactly when it's supposed to come. I don't know for sure if this book will help light a spark for you to find your own truth (if it doesn't, I hope that's because you've already found it). All I know is that finding mine was the best thing that ever happened to me, and it's my soul's desire to help others find their truth too. Whether truth is referred to as our passion, life purpose, true love, our destiny, whatever you want to call it... and whether it be through this book or some other means, I believe we each have a duty in this life to find our truth.

There's one thing I know:
YOU WERE MEANT FOR GREATNESS.

Even though I might never have met you in person, I know you were meant for greatness. Your truth, your greatness, is inside of you. It's your mission to discover that greatness, and reveal it by sharing your gift with the world. It's not arrogant or self-serving to be self-aware like this: it's actually one of the most unselfish things you can do. When you live for a purpose bigger than yourself, you naturally bring people around you along for the ride, often bringing them "up" with you. You set an example of what is possible, and you become a role model; someone that other people gravitate towards, even if they're not sure why.

Your truth is waiting for you. It might come when you least expect it, but it *will* come. You are here on this planet with the potential to evolve into a better version of yourself. Nothing on this earth stays the same. Your physical body transforms itself without you having to do anything, but transformation of your consciousness takes a little more effort.

Every person has a higher version of themselves, a greater potential. If you have any doubt about your potential, I challenge you to suspend that belief, at least while you're reading this book. Your truth lies in letting go of the weight that's holding you down. Once you're on the journey of experiencing and

Introduction

discovering your Higher Self, there is no limit to how far you can go. At that point, growth and expansion become a way of life; your way of operating in the world. You continually create and re-create yourself according to whatever passion lies inside you.

This is my story of personal transformation and the steps I took that brought me to where I am now. My journey led me to realize I had a personal mission to inspire others through my thoughts, words, and actions. I've discovered that the more I try to inspire others, the more people I meet who inspire me.

I chose to share my story to encourage others to live an inspired life. The world doesn't need any more people living far beneath their full potential; it needs inspiring people. It needs you. Your inspiration is waiting, and your potential is limitless.

Choose to be an inspiration.
Choose to find and live your truth.

I encourage you to repeat the following to yourself as your personal Declaration of Truth:

My truth is out there, I will find it.
My truth is in me, I will reveal it.
My truth is a duty; sharing my truth is my responsibility.
By seeking truth for myself, I show truth to others.
I take responsibility for my truth because no one else can.
I love my truth because it belongs uniquely to me.
My truth isn't perfect; it might be messy.
By expressing my truth, I am the conduit for others to find their truth.
I will find my truth.
I am truth.

SECTION 1

SELF-SABOTAGE

CHAPTER 1

The Drunk

"Every worthy act is difficult. Ascent is always difficult. Descent is easy and often slippery." – Mahatma Gandhi

As I poured a 5 count of Captain Morgan's rum into my red solo cup, I decided to ditch the chaser and ice. I gulped heavily until I felt just the weight of the cup in my hand. It was clear I was drinking differently, as though I were on a mission: a mission that lacked morality and bred stupidity. It was a hot summer night in June and I was celebrating a friend's 21st birthday. I wasn't so much celebrating as I was heading for a place I knew well and had visited often. On this night however, I was traveling fast.

As new members of the party arrived, I made a point to be first to greet them. I cheered loudly for no reason at all, grabbing the Captain Morgan's bottle once again. "Mike! Where the hell you been!? Let's take a shot!" It was clear to everyone at the party that it would have been much better for me to dunk my face into an ice bucket rather than fuel the fire of my

Find Your Truth

drunkenness with more alcohol. I carried on however, gulping another inch pour from the cup. My face burned from the liquor as I walked up to my friends' parents who I didn't know very well. Slurring my words and talking nonsense, I felt overly confident, certain they were happy to see me.

It was probably around 11:00 PM and I'd been doing my best to stay off my phone, in fear of what texts I might send. At the time, I was in a very unhealthy relationship: it was the long distance type, where we would get jealous whenever the other would go out to party. Although drinking binges like this weren't uncommon, they were intensified when things weren't going well with my girlfriend.

Tonight happened to be the last straw because I knew she was out with an ex-boyfriend who I couldn't stand. That in itself was a good enough reason for me to hit the bottle so hard. Drinking was the only way I knew how to cope with feeling dismissed, emasculated, and betrayed. I poured another half cup of rum and went around back to take a piss in the bushes. Then...lights went out.

The next thing I know, I woke up and found myself lying in someone's front yard. This wouldn't have been so bad if two cops hadn't been on top of me, holding me to the ground while another one stood nearby with his gun drawn. One of them asked where I was from and for some reason I decided it was alright to tell him I lived in West Orange, a few towns over from the one I actually lived in. The fact is, I was just five blocks away from my house. They put me into the patrol car and I was tossed in jail for the night.

The hours I spent in the jail cell hold vague memories, but I remembered asking a lot of questions about why I was there. I also repeatedly told the police that I had done nothing wrong, although "nothing" was all I could actually remember. At the time, though, I was convinced everything I was saying was logical. My mother picked me up at the police station the following morning. You can imagine the anything-but-pride she felt watching me being released from behind bars. As I walked outside and into the car, the shame hanging in the air was palpable. At 21 years old, I had proven once again that I lacked control around alcohol. However, at that time of my life, it was beyond my maturity level to accept any responsibility. I proceeded to blame the entire episode on my girlfriend, saying "Mom, she's a bad person; this is all her fault."

The remainder of the car ride passed in silence. There was something unmistakably familiar about how I felt. It brought me back five years, when I was 16 years old and had been picked up by my Mom in a similar situation. I was at a friend's house with a few other buddies and I had singlehandedly finished off an entire pint of cheap vodka. I was caught by my friend's parents as they arrived home, so they called all our parents to come pick us up.

No one would believe I had been the only person drinking. For my friends' sake, I told their parents that yes, it was me who drank the whole pint. Because of this episode, I was awarded yet another *Best Son* trophy as the other parents looked down disparagingly on my Mom and her budding alcoholic boy.

While that experience could be written off to adolescent stupidity, it didn't seem like I grew much in those 5 years. At 21 I was then of legal drinking age, which brought with it stiffer consequences. I rode home from the police station with my mom, unaware of what had actually happened. I'd hear about what went down soon enough: I just looked forward to getting home and sleeping it off.

I woke up 3 hours later with my Dad at my side. He affirmed the fate and burden of my last name, telling me "Lou, my grandfather's an alcoholic, my father's an alcoholic, I'm an alcoholic, and now you're an alcoholic." It was as if he had stabbed an open wound with a fire poker. What could I say to him lying in bed with all the cells of my body still saturated with liquor? This situation shouldn't have come as a surprise to the man.

This series of events brought a flood of memories again, this time to when I was 18 years old. I had been drinking Old English 40's in the park, in celebration of a half day at school. 120 ounces of malt liquor later and my "lower self" thought it was a good idea to urinate in the hallway when I got back home. I probably would have gotten away with it if my Dad hadn't been watching me the whole time. Of course, I didn't remember this until he told me the next morning. Luckily, I was let off the hook with only a shaming reprimand and a stained carpet to clean.

Shame was certainly a recurrent theme in my life that originated from my infatuation with drinking to excess. As I was lying in my bed hungover more from disgust than from booze, I couldn't help but flash back to other times my alcohol use caused problems for myself or others. Many late mornings after these episodes had me swearing I'd never get drunk again, only to brush that notion off quicker than it came as soon as the next party began. Drinking never actually required a party: any night was a good time to relax and sip away into the thrill of inebriation.

Still, it was quite certain that I'd hit a new low this time. I didn't know exactly what had happened the night before, so I told myself maybe it wasn't that bad. I scanned my body to see if I could make out any bruises: I seemed to be all in one piece.

Because I found nothing obviously wrong, I concluded this episode couldn't be nearly as bad as the time I had ended up in the emergency room halfway across the country. Surely that situation would have brought more dismay to a concerned parent than the one I found myself in last night.

The worst part of this situation was that it was just the beginning of a series of negative consequences. As my life went on, the lessons would get bigger. How did I miss these early signs? I guess in the eye of the storm, you can't really see the trouble that surrounds you.

You also can't see it when you've blacked out.

CHAPTER 2

The Arrest

My emergency room story happened when I worked at a golf course in the Midwest, in a small town with a population of 2,000. That summer I shared a house with four other interns...and we sure shared it! We could be found out on the front porch drinking every night, and we welcomed anyone who wanted to join in. Word got around about the parties we threw and it quickly became the "Animal House" of Small-Town USA.

Being that we were taking over the college party scene, the local girls started taking a liking to us "new guys" on the block. It was understandable the local guys weren't as enthused with our presence. It wasn't our goal to make enemies, but we did. Our summer internship was coming to a close so we decided to end things in our natural fashion, throwing one last hoorah. Up until this point I hadn't made too much of a fool of myself drinking among the townies. I had fallen asleep in a few bars, but nothing out of the ordinary for me.

This last party that summer found me enthusiastically celebrating our time there. A few hours into the night I walked out to the front lawn, straight into a disagreement going on between my friend and a few of the local guys. My friend had asked them to come inside, to save us from any trouble with the police. They were unmoved to agree with the request however, so I decided to speak a few words on the matter. This turned out to be the wrong choice.

I don't remember much about my stay in the hospital that night, but I know I was glad I didn't have to feel that knockout punch from the middle linebacker ranch-hand who dealt it. I had been rushed to the ER after I was unable to pronounce my full name to the paramedics. To the onlookers at the party, I simply looked like the skinny out-of-towner who just got his ass handed to him by a rough and tough farm boy. I'm sure they were unaware of my drunkenness and complete lack of motor skills to handle the situation.

The following morning, the ER doctor called me to see how I was doing. He told me I had been lucky I got off with nothing major. He also said that what concerned him more than my injury was the Blood Alcohol Level of .26 he found. At 150 pounds, this number was dangerously high. I told him I had a bit too much to drink, but then lied to him, saying that I rarely let my drinking get out of control. I did all I could to get myself off the phone, thanking the doctor and hanging up. Besides the bruised jaw and headache, the consequences of that night hadn't been too bad. The parents of the boy who hit me offered to pay for the hospital charges out of fear that I might sue for more severe damages. This meant I was off the hook yet again.

Luck seemed to be a theme with my drinking escapades. Over and over again, I'd hurl myself into a drunken oblivion and come out somewhat clean. I never took any responsibility

The Arrest

for my actions and had no regard for consequences. How long could I keep it up at this pace?

The morning after my most recent drinking binge and overnight in the jail cell, I uncurled myself from my fetal position, deciding it was finally time to face the music. I walked carefully down the stairs to the kitchen, still feeling the effects of the night before. My Mom and Dad were sitting at the table, looking like they had just been planning a funeral. I sat down at the table as uneager to hear this story as they were to tell it.

I had already made up my mind that this was a regrettable situation, but that I'd just move on with life like I had done each time before. It seemed that no low could really shake me from my demons: no consequence besides that of dying could force me to slow it down. There would be an infinite number of unfamiliar places I could wake up before I'd change my ways; an immeasurable number of relationships that would be squandered before I'd realize what was holding me back.

I listened as my parents started explaining what had happened, but I didn't really hear them. I was tuning out...until I heard them use the words "attempted burglary". I suddenly realized that this wasn't just about me anymore. I had been arrested for attempted burglary.

As the story unfolded, I learned that I had left the party around 1:30 AM. People at the party said they saw me walk out back but then I disappeared without saying goodbye. What happened from the time I left the party until the time I got to the unsuspecting neighbors' house will always be a mystery. Equally unnerving was my phone log from the night. It included calls to ex-girlfriends' parents, undoubtedly making them feel relieved their daughter was no longer with someone like me. There were also texts of despair and gibberish sent to various confused recipients.

Find Your Truth

The walk I had set out on when I left the party was towards my home, only a ten minute walk away. On my way, I had decided in my stupor that it was a reasonable idea to choose a random stranger's house and start pounding on their front door. Wearing a backwards Cincinnati Reds flat brim cap while slurring, yelling, and demanding entrance to their house was enough to have alarmed even the toughest of Navy Seals. I learned later that the family in this home had more reasons than most to be concerned. They had two very young children, one of them a newborn just two weeks old. I could only imagine the shock the parents must have felt.

Noticing my thuggish look, the man of the home positioned himself behind the door, armed with an oversized chef's knife (I was told months later that he was holding nothing back, just minutes away from opening the door and attacking me). Thankfully the cops showed up first and took me away from any pending danger. Without any other reason than that I was screaming and demanding entrance into someone's home, they laid the charge of attempted burglary on me.

I could handle having been cited as a nuisance or for being drunk in public, but attempted burglary? This was no joke. Attempted burglary came with actual jail time. No longer were my actions yielding simple emotional shaming, but here was my first legitimate arrest. This should have made me clean up my act immediately. It should have been a wake-up call to tell me I was out of control. It should have caused me to make the change my soul was so desperately seeking.

It should have, but it didn't. I wasn't ready. I hadn't reached the level of maturity, or wasn't able to see the bottom when I hit it. It didn't connect for me that these actions were holding me back. Life has a funny way of teaching us the same thing

The Arrest

over and over again until we get it. I was ignorant about changing my lifestyle then: it just wasn't the time. I had my entire senior year of college ahead of me and nothing was going to slow down my endless search for the next party; not even jail time.

Considering that my motive was not to rob their home but just a belligerent mistake, I was able to explain myself to the homeowners and had the charges dropped. Unscathed from lasting consequences yet again, I moved on with life and into my senior year of college. As far as I was concerned, the party was just getting started.

Find Your Truth in My Story

You may or may not relate to some of the darker times of my drinking history. Maybe you have a different addiction, or you're leaning on a crutch you wish you could release. You may turn to food, porn, video games, or anything outside yourself that makes you feel better in the moment. Your soul knows that your dependency on that thing is causing distress in your life: however, you may find yourself in these situations again and again.

Change happens by making a new decision. Until you make a new decision in the moment, life will continue to hold you back in old situations. You'll fall back into the same pattern and lament, "Oh I did it again!" Change is an inside game. It starts by taking responsibility for what it is you want to transform. From my story, it's clear that blaming others was getting me to the same place over and over again. Blame will never serve you. Blaming only keeps you from your truth, and liberation is found only when we become responsible. This doesn't just apply to addictions, but can apply to many types of circumstances.

Maybe you're reading this book because you're fed up with your job, your mundane routine, friends, significant other, family...maybe you're just fed up with life. You may feel as if you followed the script: you bought the car, had the family, paid the mortgage. Others looking on would say you're living the good life, but you know something is missing. Maybe you worked your way up the ladder only to discover it was leaning against the wrong wall.

If this describes you, the same principles about responsibility apply. Nothing about your life is going to change until you do. You'll find yourself at the same places, with the same people, doing the same things. You'll get the same paycheck, go on the same lunch breaks, and fear Monday as if it's an apocalypse. The boredom or despair you feel isn't your boss's, parents' or girlfriend's fault. Change depends on you. You are responsible for the outcomes in your own life. Once you accept this level of personal accountability, you can then take back the control.

Examine the patterns in your life: they tell you a lot about the decisions you're making. If you don't like the patterns you see, maybe it's time to take control and change them.

CHAPTER 3

The Addict

"The greatest minds are capable of the greatest vices as well as of the greatest virtues." - Rene Descartes

If it's not clear to you yet, I'm the kind of person who likes to take things up to the next level. I've always found it difficult to have passive hobbies, or just dip my toes in the water. I have an unquenchable thirst to immerse myself in the things that give my life meaning and purpose. Deep down I believe we all do.

I believe people who can throw themselves heavily into a hobby or interest possess a quality that should be cultivated for good use. People with this quality can sometimes be labeled as having an "addictive personality". This term has gotten a bad reputation. When the mind obsesses about something every day, it's clearly focused and that thing becomes evident in one's life. An addictive personality means you let go of resistance and allow yourself to get carried away by the thing that's holding your attention.

The addictive person lets himself get lost in the beauty of a sunset. She's the one who laughs in the forest as the rain begins to pour down. The addictive person is only satisfied when they can fully experience what life has to offer. The addictive person doesn't let the fear of consequences cripple action. The addictive person knows what they want, and they do what it takes to get it.

An addictive personality can be not only favorable, I believe it's necessary to achieve what you desire. So why have we tarnished the label? Why do we preach caution to those who have this quality? We should be praising it instead.

Find someone who has an addictive personality and tell her to start a company. Tell him to find something that's worth getting addicted to. We must learn to harness that energy so that it yields fulfillment, abundance, productivity, and peace. Only when the addictive person becomes passionate about harmful things does it cause problems such as emptiness, longing, and self-sabotage.

Addiction itself isn't a problem. We are all addicted to something, whether it be caffeine, shopping, music, sugar, whatever. It's the label that doesn't make sense. For example, why do people who stop drinking suddenly become labeled as "alcoholics" when the people who drink heavily on a regular basis are considered normal? We have some work to do about how we use limiting labels, including "addict" and "alcoholic".

I feel strongly about the misuse of the term because I've seen first-hand what both sides of the spectrum look like. I understand a subconscious search for meaning that can be expressed in harmful or self-sabotaging ways. I've felt the frustration of giving so much of myself to things that weren't bringing me true satisfaction. I'm here to speak to those people who become obsessed with a thing because of the *feeling* it gives them. That's what people are often searching for, a feeling.

We act because of a perceived notion of how things will make us feel. When something gives us a good feeling, it becomes imprinted in our consciousness and we work to re-create that feeling with the same or similar experiences. This can have positive or negative consequences.

Richard Branson for example, describes one of his philosophies about business as having fun, saying if he's not having fun, it's not worth it. He associates building businesses with the *feeling* of fun. He starts on a project, working towards that feeling, and his efforts have made an impact on music, communication, and transportation (he also likes to celebrate with champagne, but his "addiction" was building businesses, not alcohol). Amy Winehouse on the other hand was one of the most talented singers of her generation, yet her addiction leaned more heavily towards alcohol than creating music. Even one of her hit songs makes mention of how she wouldn't go to rehab. Her addiction to the bottle won out.

Our will is something we can consciously control; we can use it as the compass of our life to guide us in a positive direction or become victimized by the downward spiral that many poor decisions might create. The scary part of the downward spiral is that while you're in it, you could feel very stable and in control. It's only when you move to an outsider's perspective that you can see the twisted web you wove.

I speak to this all with the firsthand knowledge of falling down the spiral and by divine grace, rising above it all to see my life objectively. This next part of my life paints the picture of that downward spiral and sheds light on some of the darker places I've been. In my search to feel all of life's joys, I found shortcuts as my most preferred method. It was only later that

I realized the shortcut wasn't found outside myself. The shortcut comes from a life force within that paves the way to what could be referred to as personal liberation.

Once you find the right wave to ride, it will take you to shore rather than crashing and leaving you unsure of which way is up. In writing this from the vantage point I am now, it's unfathomable to believe I let myself get to such a dark and lost place in my life, without even realizing that's what it was.

I hope my story is an example that shows you it doesn't matter where you've been: you have love and greatness in you. At any stage of your life, you're always just one choice away from making a change and starting the momentum rolling in your favor. If you have skeletons in your closet, let them out. Others' judgments should never deter you from being true to your nature or cause you to keep secrets from other people. Being true to yourself is the path to serenity. Many people think money brings peace and freedom. It's certainly a powerful tool when you know who you are in relation to it, but true freedom comes from breaking free from the mind chatter that holds us back from achieving greatness.

Ask yourself often what may be holding you back, and see what thoughts and ideas come up. Often it's the stories we are afraid to tell, the boss we are afraid to confront or the business we are afraid to start that keeps us trapped within the limits of mediocrity. Let us all bring these hidden things out into the open, even if they might be considered bad; this way we can finally understand the goodness in our hearts and all around us.

Here, I'll lead the way.

CHAPTER 4

The Frat Bro

"It is by going down into the abyss that we recover the treasures of life. Where you stumble, there lies your treasure."
— *Joseph Campbell*

I had always been a fan of house music (now called EDM) since I was in high school. There was something about the pulse and thrill of it that allowed me to jump all in. I loved to dance and sing my heart out simply because it felt great. It was a feeling my soul ached to express: it made me feel alive. By my junior year of college it was the number one thing I cared about. I became obsessed with the music and its culture.

Was the music popular at the time? Yes. Was my growing interest fueled by my unconscious need to feel a part of the "cool" crowd? Maybe, but there was also something so intensely riveting about it that transcended labels. When I listened to the music I would get chills throughout my entire body. It was a type of spiritual high, and I couldn't get enough. I enjoyed it so much that I let it consume my life whole.

In becoming a part of this music scene, I was exposed to the thing that's often synonymous with it: drugs. Specifically, ecstasy. I first tried ecstasy at a sweaty nightclub in the heart of New York City. I remember toasting the blue pill to my friends like it was a glass of champagne: even though I didn't feel the drug's full effect that night, I was sold.

Unlike drinking, ecstasy didn't numb my body and emotions. Instead, it heightened my senses, making me feel more alive, more aware of everything around me. Those who've tried it can understand, but for those who haven't I'll try to describe it: the feeling was like drinking a big cup of coffee while getting a massage... while in a hot jacuzzi...wrapped up in the ecstasy of falling deeply in love with someone. It allowed me to lose control but fully grasp the moment at the same time. Ecstasy only fueled my obsession with the music.

My passion for house music continued to grow after my first experience but I managed to resist the appeal of ecstasy for almost a year. Although I continued to lose control of myself with alcohol, I still had parts of a sound mind. The self who had grown up understanding the negative effects that come with drug use never would have seen himself dipping into the hard drugs college could bring. It was also that same self who made a claim that any kind of ecstasy use would be only for "special occasions." That would have been a respectable call if I had stayed true to it.

That fall brought one of those "special occasions" when one of my favorite DJ's Avicii was playing at the college arena. Word spread through the campus and it quickly became the event of the semester. It was an obvious consensus with my group of friends that we would be taking ecstasy (or "molly"

The Frat Bro

as it was more commonly referred to when it's in loose powdered form).

For the Avicii show, the molly we had was supposed to be of high "pureness". The night came and we all got ready to party, drugs in hand (well, actually in our underwear so we'd be less likely to be spotted by security). As the lights flickered and the music pumped in the arena, a rush of adrenaline came over me. It was clear I was in my happy place. We each had our bag of molly, and during the show we'd take "dips," which is when you use your finger to get some of the powder, lick it off and swallow.

This is generally a slower and safer way to ingest the drug, and it basically tastes like a sweet-tart covered in dirt. That taste becomes acquired however, once it's associated with the drug's effects. I knew it was best to take it slow because the effects could take over 30 minutes to kick in and as a powerful drug, the experience could also turn bad.

As the DJ made his way to the stage, the ecstasy started kicking in. It was as if God came down out of the sky and was cradling me like a baby. I was feeling SOOOOOO GOOOOOOOOD, like holy-moley whack-a-mole, I didn't know feeling that good was even possible. It was like "call the doctor because I'm having a major happiness seizure", like THE MOST LOVE you can possibly feel, like you can make out with your dog, you feel so good.

The hit of feeling "ecstatic" rushed over me with a soul-reaching power. My entire being filled with so much joy that I felt heaven itself couldn't even compare to it. A love that was laying dormant inside of me had come to the surface. I felt a deep connection with everyone and everything around me; a strong drug-induced sense of belonging, love, and peace.

It was evident by the head nods and smiles my friends and I were giving each other that we were all under the drug's trance. In this state of mind, all strangers are friends, and friends are lovers. We danced together in rapture that night, embracing during our favorite songs and celebrating the bond we'd formed over the past four years.

This experience was everything I could have hoped for and much, much more. I didn't know it was possible to *feel* so deeply and passionately as I did that night. "Rolling" as it's called when you're in the midst of a high, is a steady state of euphoria, and the music amplifies the experience.

As the beats of the music vibrated through the dance floor, it felt like a rumble from inside out that electrified my whole body. It was safe to say that for me, this was the definition of "ecstasy." We danced the entire night and into the morning before finally settling down.

I awoke the next day, awestruck by the experience and still feeling the love and energy. I couldn't believe it took me this long in my life before I experienced this feeling. I naively wondered: "How could there be anything negative associated with this drug?" It felt as if I had come home to a place of joy and acceptance. Where had this magic powder been my whole life? Why hadn't I started using it earlier to save me from some of my debacles alcohol use brought?

On ecstasy, there's no blacking out or losing consciousness: it's quite the opposite. It promotes a hyper-awareness and a feeling of all life's mystery and awe. Not to mention waking up the next morning in full remembrance and without the hangover (at least, I hadn't experienced one yet). I thought I had finally discovered how I could now have fun. No more making a fool of myself, slurring my speech in bars. Instead, I could feel great with music, friends, and dancing. I believed it was my ticket out of drinking myself into oblivion and causing harm to myself and others.

Find Your Truth in My Story

We all want to feel a connection, like we belong to something bigger than ourselves. It's why people join groups, root for sports teams, or go to church. It's a shared experience with people who share the same passion. We sometimes ache to feel the emotions that come along with this; to feel human and experience the highest emotions of our nature. It's what many people really want, but they're not sure how to get it.

This is an example of the first time I really felt all those emotions since I had been a child; back when I wasn't numbed and consumed with drinking every week. When I was a child I got my "highs" from something I really cared about; sports. I'm sure you have something similar you really enjoyed as a child. Think back to your childhood right now. What made you feel excited? What were you passionate about?

Many of us see our childhood as a free and happy time, when we could explore life without inhibitions or worries about "what other people will think." Guess what? You still have an "inner child" and you were meant to live life in a free, uninhibited way. You are meant to enjoy life, feeling more happiness overall rather than stress.

When I felt the effects of the drug this time, it took me back to that childhood time of pure love and happiness. My soul knew that was how I wanted to feel. Unfortunately I had been shown that feeling through a shortcut. At the time I didn't understand that I could naturally cultivate this feeling without drugs.

If you haven't felt this kind of happiness and peace in your own life, I promise...it is within you: your passions and highest states of love are laying dormant inside. It's up to you to put in the work to bring them out.

CHAPTER 5

The Raver

It was winter break during my senior year in college, two months after my epic molly experience. I was driving from New Jersey to Pittsburgh to meet up with a few buddies before heading back to Penn State for our last semester. I was more enthusiastic about this trip than anything I'd done in college so far, the reason being we were about to re-create the experience from two months prior.

While on my drive to Pittsburgh for this second event with Avicii, I was completely clueless about how naive and foolish I was being. My first experience with Ecstasy opened my eyes to new possibilities of feeling, yet it blinded me to exercising caution or understanding what was going on with my body. All I knew was that I was hooked on that feeling, and I wanted more of it.

We brought the same batch of Molly we had used at Avicii's show the time before, so we figured everything would go great. However, even though the "recipe" was the same, the actual "meal" turned out quite differently. The venue the DJ was playing at was smaller, and we weren't in our comfortable college habitat surrounded by friends and peers.

At Penn State, our experience with ecstasy felt like a homecoming, with what seemed like our entire student body at the college arena. We also had the comfort and familiarity of our frat house and apartments to return to afterward. In Pittsburgh though, everything was different. This was someone else's territory and chances were high we'd be sleeping on a beer-stained carpet sprinkled with cigarette ashes. What I came to learn during my ecstasy days is that your environment and mindset make all the difference in the experience. This particular experience was already starting off on an uneasy foot.

Although I felt different, I couldn't wait to get on the dance floor and immerse myself in the ecstatic rumble of the music. This time we were rushed, however; we had planned poorly for the time Avicii would be playing, and we hadn't realized this venue closed early.

Avicii had already started his set when we arrived. I always enjoyed the show more when I got a "feel" for the environment with a warm-up act, like the exciting climb of the roller coaster working up to the thrill of the drop and the wild ride to come. I realized I was already running late so I frantically broke out my bag of molly and went for a sizable dip. I swallowed it down, relishing the bitter taste. I headed out on the dance floor and started dancing, trying to make my way into the crowd. The only thing is, I couldn't.

The room was packed and it was tough to move anywhere. I felt anxiety hanging over me; this wasn't working out like I planned. I hoped the ecstasy would kick in so I could experience that incredible feeling again. Twenty minutes went by and I felt nothing. I started getting fretful: I didn't want to be the one missing out on enjoying our favorite songs. It seemed like my friends were already into the feeling, so I dug down into my bag for another taste. I wasn't sure how much I was actually ingesting, but another ten minutes went by and still...nothing.

By that time I was really getting restless. My friends had found girls to dance with and I was alone and sober. I tried to slow down to enjoy the experience, but I was too frantic, anticipating the ecstasy high. I pulled the drug bag out for another taste.

An hour had gone by and I was just starting to feel the effects of the drug, but it wasn't an overflow of bliss like the first time. Instead, the anxiety still loomed because of the foreign environment. The strangers in the club and the apartment where we were staying didn't offer those feelings of belonging and connectedness, or comforts of home. I moved in place in the midst of the crowd for another half hour until finally, the ecstasy and loving feeling pierced through me like a knife.

A familiar song came through the speakers and I made my way to be near my friends. I was so relieved for the feeling to finally hit me again. Like a long lost lover, it had all of my emotions wrapped around its little finger. I danced and put my hands in the air, letting the sound of the bass lift me up and carry my soul up towards the sky. I jumped, yelled, screamed and thrashed, and just as the ecstasy started surging even stronger through me, the music stopped.

It was 11:00 PM and the show was over, but my ecstasy ride had just begun. As we headed outside to catch a cab to the place we were staying, the feeling continued to intensify. I looked at my bag to see only a tiny bit of white powder left. In an hour, I had ingested almost the entire bagful, while my friends still had half theirs left. I was feeling too good in the moment to think twice about it. It was the same amount I had taken the time before, so I figured I'd be okay.

Our friends who were hosting us had decided to throw an after-party at their apartment, so we rode there. When I got to the party my ecstasy high continued to rise, and I asked a girl for one of the lollipops she had in her purse. Lollipops and bubblegum were common rave accouterment. When under the influence of MDMA, your jaw can clench uncontrollably, so having something in your mouth helps keep you from biting your tongue. The sugar's sweet flavor is also amplified on the taste buds with your senses so heightened.

I started grinding my teeth on the lollipop and headed into a room where everyone was giving each other massages. This type of activity is another under-the-influence staple which increases the hedonism of the experience. A girl began to rub my back and I closed my eyes, allowing myself to fully engage in the feeling. With my jaw swaying and eyes rolling, I lost myself and tuned out, engulfed by the ecstatic effects of the drug. I probably let myself get too much into the experience because I creeped the girl out with my incessant moaning.

As I opened my eyes and brought my awareness back to my environment, I realized I had been rolling drastically hard, way more intense than my first experience. A girl asked me if I had any drugs left and without hesitation, I gave her the rest of my bag; at least I was aware enough to know I'd had my fill. I took the lollipop out of my mouth only to notice I'd ground it into oblivion.

I desperately needed water so I grabbed an empty bottle sitting on a table and headed to the kitchen. As I stood over the sink, my body trembled and my mouth churned. I was so jittery that I found trying to talk to unfamiliar people came with a heightened sense of paranoia. A girl I was interested in asked me to go take a walk with her, but I declined. I found it difficult to form logical sentences and was becoming more aware of how cracked out I looked. It wasn't the same as when I drunkenly slurred my words; it was more like being mentally challenged with a speech impediment.

I understood how scary the situation was becoming, yet I felt trapped inside my body; I couldn't do anything to control it. I had officially crossed over to the dark side of what drugs can do. In the kitchen I was somewhat comforted by one of my friends saying, "Dude, I'm rolling uncomfortably hard" and I gave him a nod of mutual agreement. At least I wasn't in this hell alone. But I was. We sat down on the couch which overlooked the party scene and stared forward. I was trying not to look too fucked up. But I was.

I watched people giving glow-stick lightshows to each other, but I was way past the point to be able to find enjoyment in that. If anything, it was adding to the sickening feeling I had. Flashbacks of my 14 year-old self came to mind and I wondered what my Mom would think about the state I was in. The promising kid who swore he'd never touch drugs was now in a room eating his face off, eyes rolling into the back of his head.

And rolling back they were. At one point I must have looked really bad dozing away, because a guy came up to me and shook me, asking if I was okay. I don't know who it was, but that simple action might have saved my life. I didn't quite know where I was going, but if overdosing was ever in the equation, it was for me that night.

I tried to force myself to a normal awareness but it was no use. Sitting there looking out into the crowd of people, I was gripped by an intense paranoia. I felt as if I could hear everyone's conversations and they were all saying: "Look at this druggie over here." That druggie of course, was me.

The night was winding down and two people were standing in front of me. The paranoia of how I looked and the fact that I was just sitting there warranted me saying something to them, a choice I immediately regretted. My intention was to say, "Hey sorry I'm not talking right now; I don't feel so great" but it came out as mumbled gibberish of a cracked-out human being, something like "Blass beelahrmunfweeee-luhwow".

How did I get to this low place?

Finally the party came to an end, with random people passed out all over the couches and floor. The TV was on a channel playing static, like an old school television with a bad antenna that couldn't quite get reception. As I looked over this drugged-out room I was in, I again questioned how I could be there. It was evident to me this was the bad side of hard drugs I had been warned about.

When ecstasy turns bad, it feels like your mind is trapped in a horror movie. It's a self-inflicted paranoia that I wouldn't wish upon my worst enemy (I wouldn't wish it on anyone, but you get the idea). For five hours, I watched my own personalized horror film: a combination of depression and embarrassment can only begin to describe how awful it was.

I stayed up that entire night, my mind and body awake from the drug use. The molly had slowly worn off and I was relieved to see the sun, as well as my friends who were starting to wake up. All I wanted to do was get the hell out of there and go to a familiar place. I was still rattled by the horror of the experience but at least now I was able to form words and sentences.

We gathered our things and headed back to Penn State for our last semester of college. When I got back to my apartment, I lay on my bed in deep gratitude to be comfortable, away from that awful drug-induced hell. Was this experience a lesson learned? The answer was a resonant NO.

Find Your Truth in My Story

Have you ever tried to re-create a great experience from your past, only to realize it was a lot more fun the first time? Whenever you try to re-create an experience, you could be setting yourself up for failure. The reason is because you have expectations of how something should go. When that's the case, you're choosing to set a bar which gives you a possibility of being disappointed.

My experience here is an extreme example of this. I had the expectation that partying with my friends was going to be the same as it had been before, so I didn't bother to account for variables. I naïvely thought that since *most* things were the same, I would have the same great experience. If I had accepted the new circumstance as different and figuratively, "rolled" with the situation, I may have ingested the drugs slower, and the night would have turned out differently. Instead, I tried forcing it, trying to make the experience the same as I had while at Penn State.

No matter how much you might want to, you can't re-create the past. Trying only leads to boredom and frustration. Life is happening *NOW*. When you realize and actually experience life *in the moment*, you can then create each moment into whatever you want.

Finding your truth starts with this, seeing each moment as an opportunity to express yourself and have fun. You know the best times in your life are when hours seem to fly by and you didn't even realize it. This happens because you are "present" and flowing with what's in front of you. In Pittsburg that night, I wasn't going with the flow; my mind was stuck in the past. I didn't accept the present because it wasn't matching my expectations.

Where are you hanging on to expectations? How are you living in the past, or how are you limited by your mind? It may be with a family member, an experience, or even a job promotion. Try letting go of the outcome. Let go of the way you "think" things should go, and just accept what *is*. Ask yourself how you can make this moment the most enjoyable, because that's what your life is made up of: moments. You can only focus completely and intently on one thing at a time, and there is only one time; that time is now.

CHAPTER 6

The Idiot

"Addiction isn't about substance - you aren't addicted to the substance, you are addicted to the alteration of mood that the substance brings." - Susan Cheever

    The night in Pittsburgh shook me in ways I didn't know I could be shaken. Sometimes a hangover from drinking might last a few days, but it was normally a foggy, lethargic feeling. The whole week after Pittsburg I was still shaking off the experience, only this feeling was different than a drinking hangover: it was a much darker type. It was more like a depression, rather than feeling physically sick. Fortunately, I was able to get through the week and return to a feeling of normalcy. Admittedly, an alcohol buzz each night seemed like the most logical band-aid to help me forget that depressed state.
    Like most of my previous wake up calls, I didn't really wake up. I kept acting as if I were invincible because I'd been shown time after time that things just got brushed over. I was oblivious to the severity of the situations I tended to get myself in, and all I cared about was continuing to push the limits of fun

and excitement. I was hooked on the stimulation. I saw a party and asked: "how can my friends and I get the most out of it? What mix of music, booze, girls, and drugs would equate to a night we will always remember?"

I was living for the legendary experience, but living for it in all the worst ways. I was passionate about partying, and when you're passionate about anything, you create intrinsically meaningful experiences with that thing. I hadn't learned yet to explore passions that were positive, healthy, and sustainable. Moronically, I thought this type of partying could last forever.

I continued through the semester, raising the bar on "fun" whenever I could. I had only a faint memory and concern for that bad night in Pittsburgh. The parties came and went until it was time for the ultimate celebration: the epic week of widespread degeneracy commonly referred to as Spring Break. It was my first time taking part in a real spring break vacation with college friends. We booked a trip to the Bahamas along with a hundred other people from our school. It had the recipe to be one of the wildest weeks of my life, and I was breaking a sweat just from the anticipation.

As we landed in the Caribbean and waited for our bags at the terminal, we started getting the drinks flowing with some rum cocktails. I was ready to take on this week full throttle. I was elated for the debauchery of self and the endless onslaught of girls the forgotten nights would bring.

Once again I threw all caution to the wind. I took rides to the slums to pick up cocaine, or whatever the mix of chemicals it was. With cocaine it was never really about the drug itself: it was more about the excitement I got from ripping the mirror off the hotel wall to line up rails and take them down like Tony Montana. It's such an egoist drug with the false sense of self-confidence it brings, and the notion that "I'm partying harder than you are." For this trip however, it wasn't the cocaine that caused the problem.

Midway through the week of nonstop drinking, we had planned to go away from our hotel to a secluded island. The DJ Steve Aoki was playing and it was supposed to be the highlight of the week. We figured if this event was the pinnacle, then we needed to party like it. Before the trip I thought about bringing ecstasy on the plane because I knew it would be difficult to find in the Bahamas, let alone find stuff we could trust. It was a close debate, but I decided that it wasn't worth federal prison time.

I questioned that decision after what happened.

Instead of just drinking and doing lines of cocaine all day, we made it our mission to find some ecstasy. When your mind is determined to do something, the Universe has a funny way of responding in unexpected ways to help bring you that desire. This time was a classic example of me using this theory of Universal Law in self-defeating ways.

As you might guess, we ended up finding ecstasy from a local guy who was near the beach; a Jet Ski driver. He handed us the assortment of pink-hearted pills in exchange for our over-privileged tourist dollars. We were set. We scattered the pills among our group which gave me a false sense of security: I thought the day would be all I believed it could be. I hadn't eaten anything solid all day so I grabbed a couple pieces of bread from the café and headed off on a cab ride to a remote part of the island. From there we hopped on a boat to get to another island, just a couple hundred yards out.

On the boat, we discussed if it would be best to take only half the pill, since we didn't know what it was we actually paid for. Once again, ignorance won out and we decided to take the chance on going for the whole shamboozle. Like my first experience with ecstasy, we toasted the pink hearts like we were celebrating some fantastic event, washing the things down with a cup of warm rum.

We got to the island where the party was getting started. It was a square strip of land, half dirt and palm trees, half sandy beach. We arrived on the dirt side, looking out toward the DJ stage at the end of the beach side of the island. We walked into a scene of beach balls and bodies flailing. It was a perfect sunny day, and it looked to be the ideal scene, the epic Spring Break experience I had hoped for. The party had started: now we just had to wait for the drugs to kick in.

As we moved towards the back of the crowd, I felt...something; I couldn't quite understand what it was. It was nothing I'd felt before and it definitely wasn't the robust euphoria I'd known ecstasy to bring. My awareness heightened, and along with it, a sudden paranoia. If being in Pittsburgh was unfamiliar, an island off the coast of Bahamas was even more so, and brought with it even more anxiety. However, this time the paranoia hit differently than it had in Pittsburgh.

It didn't cripple me to the point of being incoherent; I was able to speak well enough. I was also with a great group of friends. I thought maybe the anxiety was because I was just sober enough to question what it was that I had taken from a total stranger; something that never bothered me too much in the past.

CHAPTER 7

The Schizophrenic

"I'm not afraid of storms, for I'm learning how to sail my ship."
-Louisa May Alcott

The paranoia I was feeling made me want to isolate myself for a few minutes. I left my friends to take a seat on a bench on the grassy side of the island. One of my friends came by to ask if I was doing alright. I told him I was feeling a little paranoid, but that I was okay. He then warmly grabbed me by the shoulder and encouraged me to take in the joyous scene that was playing out in front of us.

He depicted each part as if it were straight out of a movie scene - girls moving half naked across a picturesque background of sand and surf, while a pop-up stage hosted a DJ throwing a mix of confetti and champagne out into the crowd. "Can you believe this?" he asked.

I couldn't believe it, and at that moment my mind shifted back to a positive direction. He inspired a deep gratitude and appreciation for being on this island with friends, celebrating our great college years. He encouraged me to look at what a dream the place was that we were in. It was exactly the positive boost I needed, a distraction from my concerns.

I stood up and headed back over to the party with him. I let my mind chatter subside and got immersed in the moment. For the next few hours we partied and celebrated like it was college spring break, because well, it was. I mentioned to my friends that the drug we were on didn't seem like ecstasy, but that ominous point got over-looked because now we were all feeling good. My friends agreed that whatever we took wasn't ecstasy, and shared in my ignorant bliss. The fact that we didn't know what it was didn't induce the healthy fear it should have. At least, not at that time.

We enjoyed ourselves for another hour until the party wound down and the sky grew darker. A chill swept over us, almost as a foreboding of the terror that was yet to come. As this happened, I had an awful feeling in my bones that something just wasn't right. The drug was starting to hit me like waves onto a shore. It felt very strange, like instant highs and lows coming both at once. I looked at my friends and saw that they had the same concerned look as we walked aboard the boat. It was as though we all knew something was about to get worse before it got better.

We made it to shore and hopped in a cab to go back to the hotel. I felt like there was a demon inside me that came out then hid again, about every 15 minutes. During the cab ride I was in this state of horror as the driver moved recklessly into the night. It was a 7-passenger minivan and I was seated smack in the middle. I felt some security in this, and knew there was no way I could handle the panic that being in the front seat would have brought. At one point the driver was faced head

The Schizophrenic

on with a car coming straight at us from the opposite direction. As the lights blinded me, I felt as though my heart literally stopped. In what felt like slow motion, the driver swerved out of the way just in time. All I kept thinking was that I just wanted the driver to get us back to the hotel; I didn't want to die like this. We arrived at last at the hotel and my horror subsided, but it was just a remission. A deep relief washed over me, giving me some calmness during the storm. My mind ran through all the terrible situations that could have occurred, and being out of the cold night and into the warmth of the hotel was suddenly comforting. Having the comfort of the hotel room meant everything to me, at least for the next half hour.

We headed up into our rooms and continued partying. It's tough to describe the feeling of this drug and the effect it had on me that night. It was a rollercoaster ride, taking me up to a schizophrenic high, and then down to the depths of what the gates of hell might feel like.

The night moved on in a consistent, twisted hybrid of pleasure and psychosis. At some points I felt great, and other times I felt like I wanted to commit suicide. The drug-induced low points came down on me like a knockout punch of depression and remorse. None of us really knew what to do, so we all laid in one room, just trying to wait it out. The mental ride was simply hell. The drug brought delusions of the scariest kind.

While lying in bed I looked over at my left arm. It resembled that of a junkie, covered with bruises. I immediately thought about my Mom: what would she think of this scene? What would she do if the cause of my death was taking drugs from a jet-ski driver in the Bahamas? I felt like I had miserably failed at life, and prayed that if I could just get out of whatever drug had control of me, I wouldn't let my mom down again.

I looked down at my foot and was struck with an elevated panic. It looked as though a baseball was growing out of it. Two weeks earlier I had been partying with my fraternity and during a drunken dance-off, I clipped the edge of the stage, twisting my ankle. It was bad enough that I wasn't sure if I was going to be able to make the trip. The next two weeks I put going to class on hold, nursing my ankle so I could go on the Spring Break trip. With all the movement and dancing I'd been doing, it looked as if the sprain had swollen back up.

I stood up, staring at my foot and began expressing my terror. The crazy thought struck me that I if I didn't get it checked out, my foot might need to be amputated. Once that idea got into my head, I started walking around the room freaking everyone out. I was screaming in fear, about what looked like nothing to other people. I was walking around in no pain, but telling everyone I needed to go to the hospital or my foot might have to be amputated. I was completely delusional, having lost all track of reality. My thoughts turned again to my mother: how could I have gotten myself to this point, and how many times would I live to ask that question again?

I moved around the room in a frenzied panic when it hit me: this was all a delusion caused by the drug. My foot looked no different than it had before, I wasn't in any pain, and I could walk fine. When I realized that, it was as if I had stabbed myself with a tranquilizer gun: the roller coaster again got back on its climb, and I felt a deep sense of relief. I laughed at the fright I had just caused myself. I was overcome with relief that I didn't have to check myself into a hospital in the Bahamas. All I needed to do now was escape the psychiatric ward of my own brain, which had been created by the drug.

The night continued on with these ups and downs, never reaching the low of the time I thought my foot might need to

The Schizophrenic

be cut off. I didn't sleep a wink, but it seemed like my sound mind was returning, and that the worst of the drug's effects were over.

The next morning I headed out onto the resort beach and literally kissed the sand out of gratitude for being alive and surviving the horrific experience. My friends felt the same way, and we questioned what it was that we took. Obviously we'd never know. If I had to guess, I would say it was meth, speed, and a mixture of other chemical stimulants.

Taking ecstasy from a Jet Ski driver in the Bahamas was easily the dumbest thing I'd ever done. What happened on that trip was the epitome of what parents and teachers warn students about. Just how stupid could I be? How many dances with the devil would it take for me to wake up?

The worst night of my life which we dubbed "The Pink Heart Massacre" was promptly followed by the second worst, when we all got violent food poising. These were by no means even in the same league. If you've ever had food poisoning, you can understand how bad that second night was. I would take a hundred nights of food poisoning before I do another night of that pink pill.

Luckily I lived to talk about it.

Sadly, it didn't stop my ways.

Find Your Truth in My Story

They say the definition of insanity is doing the same thing over again and expecting a different result. If you're looking for a different answer yet doing the same things, the same experience will continue to present itself. You can see how this was happening in my life and how it was creating extreme negative circumstances. I'll bring this point up again later, which will make more sense when I talk about programming your mind to create positive circumstances.

If you feel like your life is a routine of stress and redundancy, imagine what the exact opposite of that would be, and focus on that.

Imagine living a life where every day you feel great and something good happens. Does thinking about that seem like a fantasy world? Good. You are living in that fantasy world. I hope to guide you to see it: to see the good and follow it, to see the light and make it shine brighter. This is my purpose and can be yours too: this is your Truth.

While your story and life experiences might be different, it's important to reflect and think about what you want, and if your actions are in line with your desires. For example, if you're reading this book, chances might be you want to find your purpose in life. Maybe this is the first book of its kind that you've read or maybe it's your thousandth. If it's your thousandth and you're still searching, maybe it's time to reconsider what you're doing. Are you reading books, trying to figure something out?

If that's the case, maybe another book isn't the answer for you: maybe you need to try something different. It's clear that the actions you're taking have continued to create the same result over and over again. If this describes you, I want you to put this book down and do something different. *You already have the answers inside of you.* Take some time to yourself in nature and see what it brings. Go do a physical activity you've never done before. Allow yourself to get inspired (in *spirit*) and tap into what *you already know.*

If you're just starting on the path to finding your life purpose, it's important to be aware of the cycles in your life. Finding your Truth may involve breaking cycles that just aren't working anymore.

CHAPTER 8

The Dreamer

"Someone I loved once gave me a box full of darkness. It took me years to understand that this too, was a gift." – Mary Oliver

You might be thinking to yourself, "Here comes the part where Lou finally turns his life around." At least, that's what I would be thinking if I read a story like that. The fact that I'd lost control of so many situations should have been a clear sign that it was time for a change. Where was this road headed?

You also might be thinking that all I cared about was partying, and that there was no way I was on a path to a productive career. That's where you might be surprised. I went to college to study PGA Golf Management (yes, that major actually exists, and it's the reason I was drawn to Penn State, where students can actually become golf professionals) and graduated just skimming a 3.5 GPA. As far as school went, I always excelled. In fact, I seemed to excel at most anything I set my mind to: it was because of my obsessive personality, always pushing myself to achieve.

My interest in golf started when I was 15 and it was love at first swing. My "all-in" nature took over and I joined my high school golf team. I was excited about the thought of dominating the sport, and I challenged myself to perfect my skills throughout high school. From the time I was a child, I never believed I'd work at a job that made me miserable. I had this deep self-understanding that I was going to do something I loved, and I would somehow leave a mark on the world.

These childhood dreams were often connected to sports as I pictured myself in legendary pressure situations. For example, I remember so vividly being a 7 year old playing an imaginary game of baseball in my backyard. I visualized the peak scene, Game 7 of the World Series, bottom of the 9th, down by one with bases loaded and full count. Guess who was at bat? I imagined that I stepped into the batter's box, giving a nod to the pitcher. My arms swayed steadily, my gaze was fully zoned in. I was completely in the moment and ready to perform in front of thousands of fans.

As the pitcher started his windup, I could already see the ball down the plate before he let it go. It's as if I was manipulating the pitch he was throwing, just with my thoughts. Heck, I knew the outcome before I even stepped up to the plate, before I had even laced up my shoes for the game.

The pitch was delivered exactly as I anticipated, two seam fastball mid height over the outer portion of the plate. With absolute certainty I leaned my weight towards my right side and then, like a lioness swiftly pouncing on her prey, I laid my bat through the plate and made contact, mid pine.

The Dreamer

The ball made its way towards right center field and there wasn't a doubt in anyone's mind about what was going to happen next. The crowd erupted in cheers while I threw my hands in the air and made my way around the bases.

The scoreboard flashed in bright lights: *Walk-off Grand Slam by Lou Redmond!*

I closed my eyes then ran around my backyard as if it were Yankee stadium. To that 7 year old boy, it was: I could smell the crisp fall air and hear the crowd chanting, LOOOO-OUUUUUU. I was engrossed with each glorifying step, completely in my own state of bliss.

That boy was thinking big. He was set on greatness. Without a doubt in his mind, he knew he wanted to do something big with his life. That boy knew he was going to be in high pressure situations, showcased on a world stage, playing it larger than life. He knew it.

But my environment changed things; the influences around me darkened that light.

My big dreams changed throughout my childhood, but they all shared one common theme—I was going go the biggest I could. Whatever I ended up doing in life, I knew I wanted the ball when the game was on the line.

High school began and so did my anxiety about fitting in, doing what others were doing. I was lucky that I found golf and the Penn State professional golf major, because I see now it was the little kid in me who wanted to do something he loved. I loved golf and I had found a way to make it the main part of my life. However, that dream world didn't last long.

While in college, I discovered that becoming a golf professional wasn't what I had thought it was going to be. It became clear that I wasn't going to school to join Tiger Woods on the

Find Your Truth

PGA tour. The common trajectory for graduates was to become a professional who worked at a golf course or country club. I learned quickly that it was a lifestyle comparable to an indentured servant. It required long hours, offered low pay, and at some places, employees were treated like second class citizens. I would be beckoning to every call of the rich whose money sometimes became a part of their lives before they were able to develop manners.

It became clear to me that I didn't want to work at a country club: I wanted to be a member. In college I felt like the lone wolf among my friends. Most of them were pursuing business degrees which seemed to hold promising and lucrative careers. I looked around me, saw what everyone else was doing, and felt like I should follow. There's comfort in following because you always have other followers to confide in. Blazing your own trail is the scary option because there's no one beside you. That's why it's so important to surround yourself with other trailblazers when you begin to walk your own path.

I didn't have the mindset of blazing my own trail while I was in college. I was already committed to a major so the option of changing was quickly eliminated due to time, effort, and expense. Although my major wasn't the most demanding, it was important for me to show up and succeed. I believed that if I could just do well in college, it would open other doors for me.

Seeing how most of my friends were going to work for companies after graduation, I figured that's what I would do too. My mind was made up to work for a golf company, which would be my ticket into the business world. Another big factor for me wanting to move into the corporate world was so that I could have weekends off. I knew I wasn't a fan of going into work Saturday hungover, or having to curb my partying due to weekend work obligations. I wanted so badly to work during

The Dreamer

the week so I could use my precious weekends to fuel my need for fun and excitement.

I set my sights on San Diego because the city was home to four of the big players in the golf manufacturing industry: I also couldn't think of a better place to go right after college. I was determined to find some kind of position that would get my foot in the door with a company. When you want something and believe you will get it no matter how many times it doesn't work out, eventually you will get it. I was turned down by a few companies until I finally got my opportunity.

I moved out to San Diego and began an internship with a company that seemed like it would be a good fit for me. I wasn't sure what I'd be doing for the internship, but I didn't care; I was just excited to be working in an environment that involved the game I loved. More importantly, I would be free on the weekends to party.

Just as college was ending and I was about to start this next chapter of my life across the country, something happened that often does when you least expect it: I fell in love.

Find Your Truth in My Story

There's undoubtedly a time in your life when you felt like you didn't fit in. I can bet that feeling was uncomfortable. You might have taken action to try to change it. Most people don't like feeling different: it can be lonely. We all have a need to feel like we belong or that we're a part of something. For me, I ended up following the crowd without giving it serious thought: it's just what everyone else seemed to be doing, so I followed suit.

The people you surround yourself with play a big factor in your values and the choices you make. I'll discuss this in detail in later chapters, but understand that if you go against the crowd, it will initially feel uncomfortable. People will judge you for trying something new and they'll try to keep you where they are. Like Mark Twain said: "Whenever you find yourself on the side of the majority, take time to pause and reflect."

Are you trying to fit in? Are you looking for the same type of job as your friends, or are you a trailblazer? Chances are if you're reading this, you're a trailblazer: you want to create something big, you want to go all-in on life, and you want to create a life you don't need to escape from.

Does it seem that most people around you have that kind of life? If not, then it should be clear that following the crowd isn't the way to go. Fortunately, it's not too late. It's never too late. You are where you are in life right now for a reason. You're being led to great opportunities, your passion in life, and your highest state of being. It's in this realization that you can open yourself up to see what's right in front of you.

CHAPTER 9

The Womanizer

It was my sophomore year of college when Kelly and I first met. I was hanging out on the porch of my fraternity house, and my eyes caught hers as she walked through the door. Some people say when you meet that one special person, you'll know it at first sight. In this case, that statement proved to be true. Something inside me knew she was different than any girl I'd met before.

She had a certain vibe that was unlike the typical sorority girls I was used to being around. She smiled with grace and had the body of a gymnast. My initial thought was, "this is the girl who will be my girlfriend." At the time she was dating someone else, not surprising for a woman like her: that only made me want her more.

By the time I had graduated high school, I couldn't contain the excitement about the onslaught of women I would meet in college. I had been successfully brainwashed with the Alpha Male Ego. Thanks to the Internet and LimeWire, I had quite a filthy mind from the time I hit puberty. I thought college would be a time of rampant sexual expression, the sleazier the better. I had dreams of drunken threesomes and late night sexcapades. Whatever innocence and sensitivity I had, it vanished that first year in my fraternity. I became the typical womanizer. Even if Kelly had been available, I really didn't deserve to be with a woman like her.

As my partying escalated through college, so did my insecurities. My need to fit in and be accepted continued to grow, and the validation of having sex with women seemed to be the fleeting cure. Waking up in the morning, then chatting campfire style with the bros was all the reinforcement I needed to make it through.

"Bro! Did you bang her last night!?"

We would all keep tallies and make games out of how many girls we could sleep with. It was degrading for all of us and now that I think about it, downright shameful. At the time, I didn't feel any shame for many of the things I did though. Nights came and went with a blur, waking up unaware of where I was, next to women I didn't even remember talking to.

The poor judgment didn't stop there. Rarely did I concern myself about protection from STD's and if I did actually have a condom on hand, my inebriated state made it impossible to use it effectively, so, I just didn't. I was extremely careless...and lucky to have escaped severe health consequences.

Kelly and her boyfriend broke up, but she was still untouchable for someone like me. She didn't know graphic details about my sexual encounters, but she wasn't blind to them either. We were among the same group of friends throughout the remainder of college, so she'd heard plenty of rumors. That's why I was so shocked the night we shared our first kiss.

Admittedly, it wasn't the romantic ideal scene with me walking her home to the doorstep after a date, locking eyes, then wondrously embracing with music playing in the background. The scene was much less Shangri-La. Instead, we were dancing in her apartment late after a night of drinking. We kept inching closer to each other until, the grace of God must have fallen on me, and we kissed. As we locked lips, I couldn't believe this unicorn of a woman was interested in me.

The kiss didn't turn into anything more serious that night and I wasn't even necessarily looking for that. I was so lost in the moment, and that was all that mattered. We ended up both passing out in her living room on separate couches. When I woke up, I noticed she was gone. Elated but confused, I walked back to my apartment with a boyish glee, running into my friend's room to share the news as though I was telling thim about a hidden pot of gold I had found.

That night began a slow and steady courtship. I caught the love bug hard, and continued through the end of the semester to swoon over her in ways that clearly showed my infatuation. My persistence and gentle-heartedness paid off, and just as the school year ended and college came to a close, we were both head over heels in love.

Find Your Truth in My Story

Have you ever gotten something you didn't think you deserved, or maybe something came your way by surprise, or in a way you couldn't explain? You might say you just got lucky; you were in the right place at the right time. Did you think it was influenced by a Higher Power? Maybe, maybe not.

From my current vantage point I can see the grace of Kelly and I coming together. We met during a time in my life when I felt I didn't deserve someone like her, and she's been there to support me while I've grown into the man I am now. It hasn't been the smoothest road, but it's definitely been the right one for me.

This principle applies to challenging situations too: it's sometimes a difficult concept to grasp, but try to imagine all situations as happening in your favor - whether you think those things are good or bad. Assume that everything is working itself out in perfect order, no matter what is happening in your life at the time. Change how you look at a situation and you'll find yourself flowing with the current instead of trying to fight your way upstream.

Try it today when someone cuts you off in traffic, or gives you a nasty remark. Look at it in a compassionate way and trust that these things are all for your benefit. It will take practice, and if all it does is make you happier and more at peace, wouldn't it be worth a shot?

CHAPTER 10

The Druggie

"Our lives are a sum total of the choices we have made." – Wayne Dyer

Not long after graduating from college and moving to San Diego, I moved into a neighborhood called Pacific Beach, or "PB" as it's more commonly referred to. It's a melting pot of young adults in college as well as new graduates; students who want to live the proverbial idealistic California lifestyle.

PB was an area I already knew well from my first few months in San Diego. Weekends were spent crashing on couches and pulling drinking benders that mirrored college life. I felt right at home with the heavy partying and emphasis on a wild time. On Sundays, big name DJs would play at pool parties and beach-like raves, which resulted in many rough Mondays at work.

The most significant event during this time was that Kelly moved to San Diego so we could be together. Only six months of dating, and she uprooted from the only home she'd ever known to drive clear across the country. She moved in with me and two other guys in a 3-bedroom apartment just a few blocks from the beach. Finally I'd have the love of my life with me to take in all that California had to offer.

Sadly though, everything revolved around partying. While I had told myself that I'd save doing drugs for just the big events, this changed as soon as I moved to San Diego. I used slightly more caution, but ecstasy continued to be a big part of my life. The circle of friends I found myself in consisted of people who shared in this habit, as well as a few drug dealers who fueled it. I was always a head nod and ten dollars away from the thrill of the pill. Drugs seemed to be casually prevalent in San Diego, at least for the people around me.

Kelly moved to San Diego with plans of attending grad school for a Physical Therapy degree. Although not as obsessed with partying as I was, Kelly would join me, but once she was accepted into grad school, her priorities shifted. Mine didn't waver for a minute. I don't know how she stayed focused on her schoolwork during my nights of partying. There would be nights a few friends and I would be sitting around the couch, doing lines of cocaine or breaking up rocks of molly while Kelly kept her head down at the desk nearby, studying for her doctorate. She was the saint among sinners.

I was so passionate about the rave scene that I planned my entire life around the next time I'd be rolling. I spent all of my disposable income on drugs, alcohol, and clubs. I was going deeper into the rabbit hole, though when I was in it, it didn't seem like that was the case. It wasn't enough for me to just hang out with friends and have a few beers on the weekends. I felt a void for excitement that could only be filled with bigger parties and more drugs. Sometimes the parties wouldn't measure up, but the drugs would always be there.

The Druggie

An additional step to my typical body pat before going out was now a weekly ritual: "Phone, Wallet, Keys, Ecstasy." Ecstasy could be substituted for cocaine on some weekends. I considered it the lesser of two evils because of the depression ecstasy caused.

I continued to chase the high of my first ecstasy experience, but it never came. I found out first hand that what teachers and parents warn you about drugs is true: the more you use them the highs become lower, and the lows follow suit.

Ecstasy electrifies the body, putting serotonin and dopamine into overdrive. Picture a light bulb getting more power than it needs. The light burns bright, but also burns out quickly. An ecstasy hangover works the same way, burning through serotonin only to leave the brain depleted of it. The effects of this drug led to intense bouts of depression and anxiety for me on the mornings after rolling. Depending on the amount I had taken and my overall experience, my ecstasy hangovers could last up to a week. During these times I would feel vaguely depressed, like my body and life were flat, empty and lifeless.

I thought a lot about my habitual behaviors and their consequences, but I always wrote the dark times off as a part of the deal to get the highs: it was the price I had to pay. I did my research to try to combat these hangovers, even buying products that were supposed to fight the depression and help restore my brain chemistry to normal, but they never fully did the trick.

What concerned me at the time (and petrifies me today), is how common it was to see high school students at some of the events I attended. Standing next to a 17 year old who's rubbing Vick's Vapor Rub on himself, telling everyone how hard he is rolling is chillingly sobering. Seeing this would put my own high on pause for a moment, and I'd question what the hell I was doing there. At what point would I be too old for this? I could see the dysfunction and self-sabotage in other people but I couldn't see it in myself.

Some of the people I would hang out with were pushing 40 and still heavy into the partying scene. I'd be in clubs at 6:00 A.M. and see what looked to be a 55 year old man cracked out on who knows what, pupils the size of a quarter. Is this what I want my life to be like in 20 years? Not only did I think it was a pathetic lifestyle, but how could I sustain it? What would my brain look like with this kind of abuse that far down the road?

Even now I sometimes wonder, what has it already done? Hundreds of pills and powders later, and I might not know their true effects until I'm 60. My experience with drugs had served a purpose though; it showed me the shortcut to a feeling I would eventually learn to generate naturally. It gave me a reference point to understand some of the experiences that would be coming in my future. The only thing I needed to do was decide that I wanted to change. How many wake up calls would it take?

CHAPTER 11

The Drugged-Out

"If you wish to reach the highest, begin at the lowest."-
Publilius Syrus

After two years of living in San Diego, I was heading deeper down the rabbit hole. The Saturday of Memorial Day Weekend around 5:00 PM I was still hungover from the night before. It had been spent aggressively doing cocaine and Fireball shots before heading out to a club downtown, where the shots continued into the night. Music pulsed, lights flashed, and I danced with anyone who seemed like they wanted to. As sweat poured down, I ripped off my shirt and let myself move with even less inhibition. I continued into the night in a drunken, cocaine fueled haze.

My body was tired and urging me to take a break, but it was one of the biggest party weekends of the year. I also had free tickets to an EDM event that night, and I had just picked up a large amount of molly from my neighbor earlier that week. The recent batch proved to be good and it was relatively cheap (when I found a bargain I always took the opportunity to stock up on party supplies; I liked to have it available).

Having drugs stashed in my room gave me a sense of security. It's the kind of satisfaction you get from going to Costco and buying your favorite food in bulk. It's nice to know that it's there for you when you need it. The problem was that when the weekend came and I knew I had drugs on hand, I would seldom have the discipline to save them for a "better" time. Therefore, every weekend gathering was enough of a reason to indulge again.

I had become a casual user. Drugs didn't have to be a part of the whole night: maybe just a lick before heading out, or a small dose packed in my pocket to have with a drink at the bar. For me it was just something to "take the edge off". It started out innocently enough but the more often I did it, the more habitual and essential it became. The times I didn't have drugs stashed away made me feel unprepared. I felt like I would be left out if something awesome was going to happen, and I didn't have a way to take it to the next level.

This holiday weekend I was fully stocked and free show tickets didn't come along every day, so I moved past the hangover and texted my friend to see if he'd be up for the show. After receiving an enthusiastic yes, my energy level rose and I began preparing for the night that lay ahead.

Preparing for a night out was more thoughtful in my earlier, infrequent days of drug use. I used to put more energy into the pre-planning process. Lists were made of all the odds and ends I would need to heighten the experience, and plans were thought out weeks in advance about what we would do after the show. I would even change my diet the week before so that I could best prepare my body for the extreme ride I would be putting it through.

The Drugged Out

The more frequently I used Ecstasy though, the less these plans seemed to matter. Instead of becoming a novelty, it became a commodity. What started as an experience that I once reserved for special occasions with my best friends was now being used while I met new "friends" in clubs and through drug dealers. It was clear that the people I was attracting into my life were becoming increasingly less the type of person someone would want to introduce to their parents. While you're in the middle of a situation like that though, it's tough to see it for what it is.

It was normal to get texts from drug dealers alerting me about a new batch they'd just received, or calls from people I met at a rave, asking if I wanted to come to their hotel room to do cocaine. Some of these party-goers even had children waiting for them at home.

I look back at situations like this and the various new people coming into my life, and I can see how my mind shaped my environment, which then reinforced my mind. This is before I had heard anything about the Law of Attraction. It's so clear how I was using both my will *and* this Universal law to bring these kinds of people and situations into my life. It was during this time that I started getting a strong visceral feeling in my gut, telling me something wasn't right.

Every week that passed and every party I went to brought this uncomfortable feeling. I'd push past it in anticipation of the drug high but sure enough, that sick feeling would come back, each time stronger than before. It intensified after the drug had run its course, deepening my depression from the ecstasy hangover. For days afterwards I wouldn't be able to eat or sleep well. I would look at my pale complexion in the mirror and noticed that I looked older. I felt drained of life. It seemed as if my body and mind were degenerating at a rapid rate.

No longer was my ecstasy use primed with a week's worth of hydration and healthy eating; it was now sandwiched between heavy drinking and other substance abuse. My healthy regard for my body and cautious respect for the power of the drug had been steadily declining.

This night was no different. About 9:00 pm I headed over to my friend's apartment with the bag of molly. At this point in my drug use, it was no longer effective to just take "dips" of the powder like I had with my first few experiences. Now I had to condense a bunch of it in pill form so it dissolved together, hitting me all at once. If it was available, I might complement this with dips, but I would much rather just drop another pill because I was sure about its impact.

I had the loose molly rocks but no empty pill capsules. We decided to empty some vitamin C capsules and use the casings to fill with molly. Normally when packing up pills it's smart to know how much you're putting in. To assist in this process a scale is used to measure the amounts, but we didn't have one at the time.

Being no stranger to packing up pills, I figured I had a good eye for what this looked like. As my friend's girlfriend looked on warily, I discerned the rock sizes and packed them into eight capsules, each with what I estimated to be .2 grams. Two for each us should do the trick, and a third should be more than enough. I packed a fourth just in case, or to be used for the next occasion.

We crushed a couple Miller Lites before catching a Lyft to the event, which was at a beat up arena in the Midway area of San Diego. In the line to get in, we saw an eclectic variety of human species: the common theme was girls wearing as little as possible. This attracted older men who attended these events for the sole reason to gawk. On many occasions I saw older men walking around at these events, creeping on the

The Drugged Out

young eye candy. In addition to these groups of people, there would be every type of drug dealer and user imaginable, ranging all age demographics.

We got inside the arena and headed out into the crowd. I'd reached the point that was no longer overcome with excitement when I first saw the lights and heard the music. All of this had become too familiar. The only thing that seemed to bring excitement and joy is when the drugs kicked in. The rest of the time was simply time to be endured.

We took our first pills and waited it out. I could still feel the partying from the night before, but was hopeful the drugs would do the trick. The high came and went quickly, so we both took the second pill while talking with a group of people nearby.

It's common for people to be friendly at raves because they're feeling so good. Many times in the past, I would make what seemed to be new best friends, only to never see or hear from them again once the night was over. I'd reached the point where this didn't interest me anymore. I found myself not wanting to talk to the people around me because I saw it for what it was: a shallow, fleeting, drug-induced communion.

The wave of the second pill's effect came and went, and without hesitation we both decided to drop the third pill. We made our way through the crowd to get closer to the front, something I generally didn't like doing. I preferred to have room to move and dance: the closer to the stage you go, the more squished up next to others you are, which tended to sober me up.

I started talking to someone next to me and we made somewhat of a quick friendship. He asked me how old I was and after telling him I was 24, there was a look of surprise on his face. I returned the question, and when he responded with 20,

I felt like I might as well be the 50-year-old I had seen in the back. His age didn't shock me because there were kids there even younger than he was, but for whatever reason, I felt like I got some twisted personal revelation. I immediately left the kid and started to think about whether or not I was getting too old for this.

I mentioned this to my friend during a trip to the bathroom, but tried not to let it distract me from the rest of the night. I wasn't sure if it was my encounter or just the drugs themselves, but even after three pills, I still wasn't feeling much. This was a sad point I'd gotten to; numb to the effects of a drug that once were so elevating.

CHAPTER 12

The Bottom

"Every experience in your life is being orchestrated to teach you something you need to know to move forward." - Brian Tracy

Ever since that first college night with ecstasy, I'd been chasing that same sort of high, but it never came. It brought only a fleeting enjoyment, but also an enduring despair. It had really been nothing more than a downward journey to this point.

Since we had it with us, we both went ahead and dropped the fourth pill. According to my estimate it was a total of .8 grams, but we couldn't really be sure. If it was pure MDMA, we should have been out of our minds. We chalked it up that the stuff must not have been very good, and hoped this last pill would do the trick.

As the night continued, the fourth pill kicked in along with paranoia from the other three. As the feeling washed over me, it was as if an anchor had been thrown down: my body seemed cemented to the ground. Enthused dancing was replaced by a slow side-to-side sway, accompanied by a hyper-negative awareness and insecurity.

With every person I looked at, I felt as if they were laughing at me. My experience turned from fun to fear. People's large pupils made them look like threatening hyenas, and I couldn't find any enjoyment in the music. The dark side of my mind had taken over, coupled with that familiar visceral discomfort that something wasn't right.

I'd been in this state of mind too many times to count. What started as a joyous celebration with dozens of my college friends had turned into a consistent vehicle to cracked-out schizophrenia. All the fun and love I once associated with raves had washed away to a doomed search for something that just wasn't there anymore.

My serotonin levels had been fried and my body was desperately trying to tell me something. It seemed to scream "THIS IS NOT GOOD!" but I wouldn't listen. If I gave this drug up, what fun would I ever have to look forward to? What kind of boring life would I lead? Wasn't the whole point of me working 40 hours a week so I could have the money and time to enjoy life? I believed nothing else could possibly bring the excitement ecstasy had.

The thought of quitting made me think of the ending scene in *Goodfellas*, where Henry Hill had been relocated to a boring suburb. He talked about losing the excitement he once had and when there was no more action, he would live the rest of his life like a regular schnook. If I stopped using drugs, I was afraid I'd be that schnook. The question was, when would the schnook option seem better than the situation I was getting myself in?

Because the event was in an arena, they opened up the bottom floor of seats to everyone. I told my friend I couldn't be on the dance floor anymore and went to take a seat in the

The Bottom

crowd. I felt like I was a metallic wrapper in a microwave on high. My brain was fried, I was shaky and stricken with panic. I sat in my mini-hell for awhile until my friend joined me, then I persuaded him to leave.

I lay in my bed that night, fully awake until sunrise. As I looked over at Kelly who was sleeping soundly after a night of studying, something triggered inside of me. When people think of rock bottom, they might describe some of the stories already shared in this book. Many times, near death experiences or loved ones getting hurt can shake a person to their core, waking them up to finally make a change. While my low points added to the overall problem of drug and alcohol use, these type of one-off occurrences never brought me any real awakening.

My rock bottom didn't come in a hospital room or jail cell. Instead, it came from simply being fed up. I was sick of putting myself through experiences that brought fleeting joy and lasting pain. I was tired of causing damage to my brain, sucking every last bit of serotonin from it. I was losing sleep, I wasn't able to properly digest food, and I was spending thousands of dollars for a self-imposed depression that lasted for weeks: it just wasn't worth it anymore.

My rock bottom came to me as a sum of all of my experiences: it was the culmination of chemicals that pushed me further and further down a road I never realized I signed up for. The child inside who was so hopeful for the grandiosity of a life to come was aching for me to listen to him again. Only through this means could I listen to how far off the path I had wandered. I wasn't able to hear this inner child of myself loud and clear, but that night I heard a whisper.

My outer environment had kindled an inner realization. I didn't have a huge revelation or "Aha" moment; there was no radical shift. It was just as though I had been driving down a long street for years, and I had finally taken the time to notice one of the many signposts that read, "Dead End." My inevitable destination dawned on me and I realized the most obvious and best move would be to turn the car around.

I didn't feel a joy as if I had found some kind of hidden treasure, and I didn't call my parents to tell them the news. For me it was just calm, simple, and profound. On this day I simply said "I'm done."

The Bottom

Find Your Truth in My Story

Wake up calls don't always need to be big or dramatic. Sometimes it may be that you continually feel nudged in a certain direction. Is there something that keeps coming up in your thoughts, or that keeps you up at night? Are you being called to leave a relationship, get a new job, start playing an instrument? It starts out subtly at first, and waits for you to recognize it and follow what the voice is telling you.

Don't make your wake-up call wait. Listen where you are being drawn to because it's not something that will just go away. It will be there for you, waiting for you to make your move. Like a sly tiger it's always lurking, breathing stronger each day that passes, every moment you wait.

Finding your Truth starts by choosing to BE a new way. For me it was no longer being a raver, no longer being someone who took ecstasy. It is in new ways of being that we transform ourselves. Making firm decisions can open doors because it's then that you have clarity of mind. Your mind can then be free to focus all its efforts on your decision because there's no longer any confusion. Little did I know where I would end up after making my decision and allowing my mind and heart to guide me.

SECTION 2

SELF–EXPLORATION

CHAPTER 13

The Whisper

"Rock bottom became the solid foundation on which I rebuilt my life."- J.K. Rowling

Whenever you make a commitment to do something, life has a funny way of giving you hints to help you achieve that thing. When you take a stand against something you *don't* want, you open up possibilities to what you *do* want. When I made the choice that day to change my life, something buried deep in my subconscious started showing up in my thoughts and I couldn't shake it. It was like I finally knew I was ready for something else, but I had to take the first step. Through my act of committing, it was as if I was shown what my next step should be to achieve that goal. Little did I know that the next "step" was really a launching pad.

I recalled visiting my friend Jake in Los Angeles just a few months before. We had gotten into a great conversation about life. This was something new to me because at the time most of the conversations I had were limited to superficial small talk or random gossip about other people. I never had any idea how fulfilling meaningful conversations could be, the kind where you get so lost in the discussion that you lose track of time. Not only can conversations be peak flow experiences in themselves, but the level of connection that's built from them can be even more powerful.

A night of good conversation was a welcome change from being at a loud club where it was hard to talk to anyone. So during that visit with Jake, we had some good craft beers and discussed our current careers and goals.

Jake was a close friend from college, and someone who I admired and respected. He had a positive nature that seemed to make good things gravitate in his direction. He always had the ability to shine light onto a bad situation, making people see things in a different way. He was a positive influence in my life even before I understood that I should surround myself with positive people.

As the beers flowed and the conversation deepened, Jake mentioned something that planted itself successfully into my subconscious. He had only recently moved to L.A. so he was talking about all the new things he'd been doing. As we talked he became especially enthusiastic about a group he had joined.

He described it as a group of young professionals who met once a week in a boardroom to talk about a wide range of topics about life and business. He said there were about ten people in the group, all of them from different backgrounds.

There was something that stood out about the way he described the meetings: there was a sort of energy in his voice that hooked me. I asked him questions, encouraging him to share more information. He continued, saying that after the meetings he felt something he hadn't been able to find anywhere else; he explained the feeling as a fresh take on life. He

The Whisper

said an inner clarity came over him, fueling him to head out into the week and live life to the fullest.

I don't know if it was the beers or the glow in Jake's demeanor, but the idea of this group had been planted deep into my mind. It sounded like music to my ears and I was immediately and fervently attracted to it. It seemed like something that was right up my alley.

A little jealousy came over me that Jake had found something like this, until he said "I think this group actually started in San Diego. I could contact someone if you think you'd be interested in it." I understood at that moment that my impulse to drive up to Los Angeles and meet with Jake had a bigger purpose I hadn't intentionally planned.

After he said that I answered with a whole-hearted "YES", but as it is with many vocal commitments over a few drinks, you can never totally be sure anything's going to come out of it. When I got back to San Diego, work ramped up and whether I was too busy or too scared to make more changes in my life, I never reached back out to Jake to put me in contact with someone from this group.

I thought back to earlier that year when I had watched a TED talk by Simon Sinek, called "Start with Why." It inspired me to get out of my comfort zone and pitch a new idea at work. I ended up giving a short presentation to a crowd of 160. I was petrified getting up in front of everyone, and unfortunately I ended up falling flat on my face.

My presentation failure shook me, but at least I could stand proud that I had done something no one had asked me to do, and that I had been chosen to make a pitch in front of my company. This experience pushed me far out of my comfort zone and taught me a great deal.

It was this idea of getting out of my comfort zone that was re-surfacing now, and I thought back to my visit with Jake and him raving about this group. Sitting around a table with a group of strangers was foreign to me, and it sounded like a step in the right direction. I didn't know what to expect, but something in my soul knew that stepping into the unknown was the whole point. The things I was already doing hadn't been working.

I felt as though life had to have more to offer than going to work to fund my partying lifestyle. Where would that end? It finally became clear to me that it would end in a way that couldn't be good. I feared if I didn't move my life in a positive direction, I would eventually reach the point of no return.

The meeting with Jake had struck a chord in me and planted a seed in a back corner of my psyche. I could continue in my ways, keeping the seed dormant and eventually letting it die, or I could follow my intuition, the feeling that whispered to move in the direction of things I wanted, even though they scared me.

I was nervous about reaching out to Jake and putting the wheels in motion, but I knew it had to be done. After three months of hesitating, I finally contacted Jake and got the introduction I needed to join this group in San Diego.

I could not have been prepared for what would be in store for me or how profoundly it would alter the course of my life.

Find Your Truth in My Story

I think it's safe to say that most people want to feel good; they want to feel inspired, alive and at peace. Can you think back to a time when you felt like this? Have you left a conversation inspired then did nothing about it? Have you gotten excited about something only to never take action on it?

The Whisper

The things that inspire and excite you come up for a reason. They are your signs that read "ACT ON THIS NOW." It's up to you to interpret them. Have you ever gotten excited about something then made up every reason why you couldn't do it? Maybe you got the urge to take an Improv class then backed out. Maybe someone attracted you and you wanted to talk to them, but you got scared of what might happen.

You are always being guided to your greatest level of fulfillment. That fulfillment lies in the unknown, which is often wrapped in discomfort or fear. All you have to do is show a little courage.

Hearing about the group Jake described created an excitement in me, yet I waited three months before acting on it. I'm lucky it was still available for me. Don't waste that kind of time. Act on the things that excite you. Hesitation only leads to your story being untold.

CHAPTER 14

The Initiation

"The best time to plant a tree was 20 years ago. The second best time is now." – Chinese Proverb

It was a Friday afternoon and I was just getting home from work. This particular Friday was different than any other I'd had in the last few years. My typical Friday schedule was to leave work as soon as possible to get the weekend going. I would normally be focused on which happy hour my friends were meeting at, or thinking about what shows, raves, or clubs we would be going to during our precious two days off work.

Friday was the ultimate day at work because it held so much promise for the weekend to come. It was the esteemed 48 hour window when we were freed from our mundane responsibilities and allowed to express that freedom any way we saw fit.

Friday night was the more exciting of the two because the next day was Saturday, which meant we had two days and nights before having to go to work again the following dreaded Monday. By Sunday, there's the hangover to deal with and the somber realization starts taking hold that the next day it's back to work again. Fridays therefore, were the starting line for a weekend of letting loose and all too often, partying for 80 percent of its waking hours.

This is the reality of Fridays in the corporate world, and there was no shortage of people who shared this viewpoint about the weekends. This Friday however, was different for me. There was no happy hour lined up, and I didn't have plans that involved drinking until the wee hours of the morning. I would be attending my first group meeting that had come out of my conversation with Jake. The name of the group was "Junto."

Junto meetings were held on Fridays at 6:00 PM. When I first discovered this, as could be expected I had a lot of resistance. Six o'clock on a Friday!? How could I possibly let this take my precious time from me? I was worried that this meeting would be getting in the way of my fun. I thought it couldn't be at a worse time. Why couldn't they meet during the middle of the week? "Don't these people have more important things to do on a Friday at 6:00 PM?" These were the questions I asked myself during the week leading up to this first meeting.

Although I was skeptical about the time, I figured I should at least see what the group was about. I was nervous and timid about going to the meeting. Usually I was over-confident in situations and at times even arrogant, but in this case I felt like a teenager just before a first date. "What should I wear?" "What will she think of this shirt? "I hope she likes me…" I decided to dress business casual, hoping to portray the right "look."

I had always had a mixture of self-consciousness and vanity. I believed that if I dressed and acted a certain way, I'd be accepted. My worldview was superficial, and I believed that how I looked in front of other people was 99% of the battle. I got ready for my meeting, making sure to wear my new watch

The Initiation

and best dress shirt. Then I looked confidently in the mirror. I was nervous, but I was sure that if I looked this good, how could they not like me?

Since I imagined this would be a business-like meeting, I questioned whether I should bring a pad and pen. What if I'm on the only person who brings them? I'd look like a doofus. What if I'm the only person who doesn't? Then I'd seem like the unprepared Know-It-All. The battle raged inside my head, but I opted to bring the pad and pen. I could always hide them under my chair if no one else had brought theirs along.

As I drove to the meeting, the uncertainty of the situation washed over me. I had no idea what I'd be walking into, and didn't know a single person who would be there. I questioned why I was doing this in the first place. Why was I giving up such a precious block of time to meet with people I didn't even know? It would be a lot easier, and much more comfortable sitting at a beach bar, sipping a Margarita.

I started to regret the decision, but it was too late to back out; I was already committed. I pulled into the parking lot of a desolate-looking business complex. The building stood alone, but I didn't have a clue which door to use as the entrance point. I wandered around the building like a lost child, pulling at doors and peeking into windows. I didn't encounter anything that seemed remotely welcoming.

In my mind I had imagined a fancy executive suite at some gaudy office building in the city, but this building was in an unusual area of San Diego, mid-way between the beach and a nearby residential suburb. I wondered if this was some sort of hazing ritual for first-timers, similar to the Happy Gilmore "9th Green at 9" meeting.

Find Your Truth

I was dumbfounded, partially waiting for the perfect addition of the sprinklers coming on, when two men finally came to the door. They looked at me like a solicitor about to pitch them on switching cable providers. "Is this Junto?" I asked. One of the men said, "Yea, you must be new. Get down and give me 50 push ups." I guess I wasn't so off on the first-time hazing, but coming from a college fraternity, I was comforted by the humor. That comfort didn't last long.

CHAPTER 15

The Call, Part 1

"The opposite of addiction is connection." -Johann Hari

I was directed to a conference room so I went in and took a seat. As I waited for more people to show up, I again began questioning my choice of clothes. The two men who greeted me were wearing V-Neck T-shirts, while my khaki pants and dress shirt had me looking like I was ready for Easter dinner. I felt relieved that at least I had chosen my Puma Suede sneakers over the brown leather loafers.

The table filled up and the meeting began. Since there were two new people sitting in today, the leader of the group had everyone go around and give a quick introduction about themselves. This is where I quickly learned that I was treading in unfamiliar waters.

The man to the right of me had founded three different successful companies, the most recent being a sunglass company that had been endorsed by the likes of Diplo, Skrillex, and Tim Ferriss. Next to him was a Life Coach practicing under Tony

Robbins. Across from me sat a multi-millionaire real estate investor who during our meeting, discussed his recent trip to Neckar Island, where he had spent time learning from billionaires like Richard Branson and Sergey Brin.

Scattered around the table were six other people and I started noticing a common theme with all of them: no one had a typical 9-to-5 job. There was one guy who was working to save the California coast, and the leader of the meeting left a high paying corporate job to pursue creating the group platform I currently found myself in.

They called themselves entrepreneurs, a term I'd never really been exposed to much. Of course I knew what an entrepreneur was, but I never knew any personally, yet alone people my age who would refer to themselves as one. In my mind, entrepreneurship belonged to those who were more fortunate; the lucky ones God gifted with an idea and the ability to start something on their own.

To be honest, I thought entrepreneurs were for the most part, not as intelligent as the rest of us. When I was growing up I heard a story about a friend's parents who left their full time jobs and invested all they had to start a coffee shop. People would talk behind their backs like they were crazy to take on such a risk, and that they were making a big mistake. These opinions turned out to be true; the coffee shop failed. This is the concept about entrepreneurship that had been imprinted in my mind. Why would someone ever want to leave a comfortable corporate job? Isn't that the type of job everyone wants?

What was different about this group was not only did they seem successful in what they were doing, they were all in their twenties. How could this be possible? No one I surrounded myself with in college ever talked about starting their own

The Call, Part 1

business. Instead, all anyone cared about was securing a cubicle job somewhere and taking the first offer they saw without any real purpose behind it other than to make money. Although I was working in the golf industry, I felt the same way. I didn't care what I was actually doing, as long as it made good money. If I did, I certainly wouldn't be making collection calls like I was in my current job.

As it came my turn to speak, I felt a deep twinge of overwhelming insecurity. The group members had gone from Company Founder, Tony Robbins Life Coach, Millionaire, to me, Lou Redmond-Accounts Receivable.

I was so nervous during the meeting that I could hardly speak. I thought, "What the hell am I doing here? I don't belong at this meeting." I felt inferior to others in the group, like my being there wasn't worth their time. I'd never felt so insecure in my life.

This wasn't your typical business networking discussion. No one had an agenda. Instead, people talked about what was on their minds and what was in their hearts. Topics ranged from business ideas, to relationship struggles, to what books they were currently reading.

The millionaire real estate investor said he'd read 67 books so far that year. This blew my mind, because it was only June. Reading for me had always come with the burden of homework and book reports; I never saw it as something to voluntarily use in my favor. Once college was over, why would someone subject themselves to any more of it? The thought was so foreign to me, but one thing was evident - these guys were crushing life, and they were also avid readers.

If I didn't already feel out of place, what happened next sealed the deal. A member started discussing an event he went to called "Unleash the Power Within." The rest of the group erupted with excitement and they started talking about this guy named Tony Robbins, and how they had walked across hot coals.

Have you ever experienced what it feels like when someone in your group tells an inside joke, and everyone gets it but you? That's how I felt. I was so clearly out of place and I had to ask, "Who is Tony Robbins?" A silence came over the group as all eyes looked at me in shock over my question because Tony Robbins is, well, Tony Robbins. This was not easy to understand for a group of high performing entrepreneurs.

A metaphor for this may be showing up to do volunteer work at a Catholic church without any idea of who Mother Theresa is. As the energy in the room shifted, I felt sure they would start in with some kind of laughter or ridicule but surprisingly, that didn't happen. Instead, I was told who Tony Robbins was much in the same way a parent would tell a child to put their socks on before their shoes.

The embarrassment pushed me into silent retreat for most of the time remaining. Towards the end, I finally mustered up the courage to say something again. At the time, my life was a repeating cycle of work and partying and while I didn't mention the vices that led me to the meeting, I did give the group a small impression about my current world.

I talked about how every day was the same. I would wake up, go to work, watch about five hours of Seinfeld, and then do the same thing again until I could finally have some fun on the weekend. I knew in my heart there had to be more, so I spoke up and asked the group if they had any insight that could lead me in the right direction.

What came next was that pivotal advice that arrives once or twice in a lifetime; the kind of advice that makes you frightened at the thought of actually acting on it. It's usually simpler

The Call, Part 1

than you might imagine, but how many of us do the simple things, right?

The advice was this:
1. Stop watching TV
2. Start reading
3. Start surrounding yourself with the right people
4. Find ways to push your comfort zone

As the meeting came to an end, I had already knocked one thing off my list: pushing my comfort zone. That meeting basically obliterated my comfort zone and shook me to my core. I felt like I had traveled to a different planet. The people I tended to associate with didn't think or talk like these people did. In this group, no idea was stupid and there were no limits on how far you could go.

After the meeting, I decided to head over to one my favorite spots in San Diego. Sitting wide-eyed on a bench that overlooked Sail Bay, I reflected on what had just taken place. It was during this reflection that I received one of my first "calls to action" that would come throughout the next year. This one felt like Life handed me a deck of cards and asked "Do you want to play the game?" The real question for me was, did I have it in me to say yes?

I thought back to when I was a child, to a time when the whole world was ahead of me and I felt like I could do anything. I went even further back in time, to when I knew with my entire being that I was destined to do something big with my life.

Somewhere along the line, that childhood faith subsided and societal norms crept in. I learned over time to follow the rules, to fit in with the majority. This continued into college and my adult life, when I chose a major based on what would lead to a good job, taking the first opportunity that came along because that's just what people did. My mind was focused on supporting myself, saving for future retirement and being "realistic". I never questioned "Is *this really what I want to do with my life?*"

It was clear that the people in this Junto group didn't think like that. It was safe to say "realistic" was not a part of their vocabulary. They were commanding from life what they wanted, and not accepting any substitutes. The thought of living a dream life never occurred to me. I had always thought I wasn't lucky enough to have been dealt that kind of hand.

I had to dive deep within myself to ask my soul, which I'd neglected for so many years: "Could that be me?" Could I be a man who controls his destiny? As I asked myself these questions, the childhood flame re-ignited and I was filled with a bolt of energy for life. I stood up with conviction and said to myself "Yes! Why not me?"

A feeling of lightness came over me and for the first time in a long time, I felt free. I had no idea if I'd be welcomed back to their group, but I didn't care. On this night, a paradigm shifted and a new me was born. On this night, I decided to be the captain of my own ship. I decided to say Yes to life.

I gave myself permission to dream again.

CHAPTER 16

The Shift

"One's destination is never a place, rather a new way of looking at things." -Henry Miller

Joining the Junto group was the most pivotal decision of my life. It taught me many new things, including the core advice I received at my first meeting, which is something I continue to put into practice. Since that first day when I received the simple bits of advice, I've been able to expand on each of these suggestions. I'll discuss the steps I took and the series of events that played out in my life that eventually brought me to the place where I made such a drastic leap of faith.

As with anyone who considers themselves someone who has good advice, what they say is usually based on what worked successfully for them. A key point I learned about giving and receiving advice is if you're not where you want to be, find someone who is and listen to what they have to say.

I don't pretend to be someone who can teach you to be a marketing guru or real estate investor because that's not what

Find Your Truth

I know, but what *do* I know? I know change, I know peace, I know how to feel good. It's through feeling good that I can be my best, and it's through being my best that I will find the best thing for me to do. Finding your truth isn't about looking outside yourself for that thing you were meant to do. Outside yourself is where it will eventually show up, but the process starts from within. When you become purposeful, you attract your purpose into your life.

I've been fortunate to have been shown what happiness is, and how to choose to let more happiness into my life. I've been lucky to have learned that life isn't just a grind to endure; it's a beautiful dance to be cherished and sculpted so we can realize our highest dreams.

The ideas I share can be applied to anything you want from life. You might be craving happiness, a zest for life, or maybe a combination of both. What I'm here to tell you is that you *can* have both, and you deserve to have both. Your life - and even your children's lives or close family and friends around you – might depend on it.

So where am I on the spectrum of achieving life happiness? Why should anyone listen to what I have to say? Well, if you've read this far and it isn't obvious yet, there was definitely something that had been missing from my life and I filled that void. Maybe you're reading this book because you think there's something missing in your life too. The caveat here is that what you "think" you need most in your life might not necessarily be the biggest missing piece.

For example, how many people think they are missing love? They look for it and continue to fall into the same bad relationships over and over. What they're missing isn't love, but rather information about how they attract love based on their thoughts. As for me, I was missing a higher purpose in my life but I didn't have the information to understand how I

The Shift

could *find* that purpose. My desire for happiness and excitement led to actions that only brought me further away from the results I wanted.

Being exposed to new ways of thinking that Junto group members possessed was my "S.O.S." in a bottle. I didn't know where it came from or why it hit me so hard, but it was the means of entrance into the reality I now claim as mine. My life today is drastically different from the one you've read about so far in this book. That's precisely why I'm an expert in one thing: personal transformation.

The definition of transformation is "to change completely and usually in a good way." People often run from change like the plague. They do the same things every day because it's what they know, and it's what is most comfortable for them. If you asked them they would tell you they don't want to change. "This is who I am," they'd say.

All of us as humans have arrived where we are today because of evolution. The early Neanderthals probably didn't think they would become anything different, capable of complex thought, speech, and reasoning, but just look at the evolution that has since taken place. My point here is, how do we know for sure that it's a true statement when we say something like "This is who I am."? Do you ever wonder if there are parts of you sleeping or lying dormant, just waiting to wake up?

I didn't know there were dormant parts like that in me, but I learned hard and fast. There is a greater version of you too that you might not even be aware of. This will always be true, and how exciting is that? Change is the only constant in life. Once you understand this, you can use it in your favor. You can then consciously allow yourself to transform. If you're not transforming and evolving into a new version of yourself, you're depreciating or at the very least, stagnating. Imagine yourself as water. Stagnant water becomes cloudy and unappealing. Flowing water is fresh, clear, and enlivening. You are meant to flow.

What do you want from life? It's an unfortunate truth that the majority of people don't have a specific answer to this question. If you are one of them, how can you even start to put yourself in the direction of attaining what you want? Life won't give itself to you as a gift, wrapped with a bow on top; you're going to have to go out and get what you want. The good news is that it's never too late to do it.

Personal transformation is by no means an easy process, but once you find yourself on the path you'll be amazed at how fulfilling your own journey will feel. The phrase "it's hard following your dreams" gets passed around a lot and I understand why, because it *is* hard. It takes work to contemplate the deeper questions of life, and move through your unique journey.

Once you start though, there's no better satisfaction in life that could possibly compare. It all starts with awareness, and a shift in your mindset. By choosing to read this book you are already on that path. It's my hope you take action like I did, and that you realize the dreams you might have had as a young child are still possible. Allow yourself to dream big, and watch where those dreams will take you.

CHAPTER 17

The Mind

"When there is no enemy within, the enemies outside can do us no harm." – African Proverb

Before I was exposed to people who were living life to the fullest, I had no idea how much time I had been wasting. Wasting is actually an understatement: I wasn't putting any value on my time whatsoever. I'd become a zombie when I got home from work, watching hours of TV and mindlessly scrolling through social media. I was just focused on getting through the week, waiting for the weekend.

It was recommended to me in the Junto meeting to stop watching TV. This seemed like an insurmountable task at the time. How could I just stop watching TV? Everyone I knew watched a lot of TV and I'd always considered people who didn't watch TV as "weird." That's when I asked myself, "Self, do any of your friends run successful businesses and have the freedom to travel and do what they want, when they want?" The answer was a resounding no.

I came to learn that what you program your mind with will ultimately program you. If you feed it meaningless, drama filled reality shows, your life will be filled with drama. I entertained the idea that maybe these guys knew something most of us didn't, but I needed something to fill the time previously used for watching TV.

My first key take-away was that I needed to start reading. I had a list in front of me from the first meeting with almost a dozen book titles. When you don't know where to start, it's best to just start somewhere and see where it goes, so that's exactly what I did. The next day I ordered my first three books on Amazon: *Miracle Morning by* Hal Elrod, *Losing Your Virginity* by Richard Branson, and *Outwitting the Devil* by Napoleon Hill.

My plan was to read *Miracle Morning* first because that's the one that came so highly recommended, and one that could help jumpstart a new life. However, Amazon and FedEx had other plans. *Outwitting the Devil* arrived by itself a few days before the other two. I didn't plan on wasting any more time so I dove right in. The book was my first glimpse into the power of reading words that could connect with me on a visceral level. Like a drug, I was hooked.

It was the first time in a long time that I had been mentally stimulated in that way. I lost myself in Napoleon's story of overcoming fear and self-doubt; his epic conversation with the Devil captivated me. *Outwitting the Devil* was a gold mine of self-realization. As I read, it seemed like beams of light would go off in my head and I would exclaim, "Yes! It's so obvious." It's as if my soul was crying out, saying, "I've been waiting for you to rediscover this, it's about time!" It seemed that every other line I read, I wrote something down in a notebook because I found it so profound. I found that the most powerful

The Mind

books don't teach you anything new: they just bring to the surface those truths you already know deep inside.

Outwitting the Devil teaches that you are in complete control of how you use your mind and the beliefs you feed it. This book was my initial guide to self-mastery. Napoleon Hill explains in the book that only 2% of the population ends up successful: the other 98% are trapped by fears and negative beliefs.

I really thought about this one, only two percent? How could that be? Then I thought about all the people I had known in my life and it made sense. I thought back to those dreams I had as a child and how they were swept out of my consciousness as I grew older. Not in one fell swoop, but through the mindset I gradually adopted from my environment. I couldn't think of anyone I knew who was living their dream, or pursuing their highest potential.

Without even realizing it, other people's beliefs had become mine. My well-intentioned parents, teachers and other adults didn't encourage me to challenge the status quo or strive to live an extraordinary life: instead, with cautious tones they made clear that getting a safe corporate job was the way to a happy, or rather, "comfortable" life. All of my friends fell in line with this mindset too, which further reinforced the thought patterns that influenced my college and early post grad experiences.

Reading *Outwitting the Devil* brought me a new way of thinking but more importantly, it led me to a lifetime love affair with reading, learning, and personal growth. It opened up a world that I didn't know existed; a world where I am the one who decides who and what content I allow into my mind.

Some quotes I noted from the book are definitely worth sharing:
"Any habit which weakens one's will power invites a flock of its relatives to move in and take possession of the mind."

"You may not be able to control other people, but you can control how you react to them."

"Man has control over nothing and has no assurance of the permanent use of anything except his own power of thought."

Regarding habits, bad habits lead to more bad habits. By changing a negative to a positive, you can then start that cycle in the right direction. The last two quotes go hand in hand: you can't control situations, but you can control how you perceive them. Shakespeare said, "Nothing is good or bad but thinking makes it so." As an example, kids might see it snowing outside and say, "Yay, no school!" An adult sees the same snow and thinks "How am I going to get to work? Now I have to shovel and it will probably make me late." It's not the snow that's bad or good. If that were the case, both the child and adult would look at it the same way. It's the thinking that "makes it so."

I never realized how obvious it is to control your thoughts to make the best of every situation. I don't know why it took me so many years to learn this. I realized that college hadn't given me a great education; it was mostly to get a piece of paper and have fun. I had to wait until I started purposefully reading to learn that a self-education could be much more effective and valuable.

Like many other students, I wasn't motivated to do something just because it was required; reading became a drag for me because it was always related to homework assignments and book reports. It was just another chore that I put off. By

The Mind

the time I got my first job, I had had such negative experiences with books that I was glad that I never had to deal with them again.

Books aren't a drag when you're passionate about what you're reading. Now that I could *choose* which books to read, I read with gusto. I wanted to gain even more knowledge about things that had brought such joy into my world. I would listen to audio books on my way to work, read during lunch breaks, and eagerly anticipated filling my evenings with reading and contemplation.

I stopped being impressed by Disc Jockeys and started looking up to the world's great thinkers. Classic philosophers like Seneca, visionaries like Richard Branson, and personal success writers like Napoleon Hill became the first mentors on my road to self-discovery.

If you're in a position like I was, you might be working at a company where none of your co-workers read books. Conversations at work might be about the new House of Cards episode, or what you thought about the Monday Night Football game. I was never asked by my coworkers: "Are you reading anything interesting?"

It took me awhile to notice it, but after I started becoming an avid reader and learning so many new things, I felt like had a leg up on many of the people around me. I discovered that reading was actually changing the quality of my conversations: I had valuable things to say and I was able to pass along knowledge and information to co-workers and friends. Reading definitely had a positive impact on my work, relationships, and overall well-being.

When I talk to people about my favorite books, they often ask me which ones I recommend. I always find it hard to answer because I believe there's a natural order to how and when information comes into our lives. My usual advice is to start somewhere and see what resonates most with them.

Unlike television, reading takes mental strength and can wear you out. You may not have an aptitude yet to fill 5 hours a day with reading, especially if it's been a while since you last picked up a book. If that's the case for you, there are other ways you can expand your horizons: podcasts, motivational YouTube videos, and informative documentaries are a few examples.

Never feel obligated to finish a book, and don't read books just to keep score. Counting the number of books you read can be a good motivating factor as long as you don't get caught up in focusing on the numbers, which would be missing the whole point. Quality is subjective, so read the books that speak to *you* and don't let anyone tell you they're not good.

Read for pleasure, read for work, read when you don't have anything else to do. Read a lot and then don't read at all. Read because you're blessed to be able to. Read, then question what you're reading. Read books that have opposing beliefs, just so you can be educated about both sides of an argument.

Albert Einstein said that imagination is more important than knowledge. It's my belief that they're related; knowledge allows the imagination to grow and become inspired. Reading was a core building block to a new and fulfilling life for me. Since you're reading this now, it's my hope it will be for you, too.

CHAPTER 18

The Right People

"You are the average of the 5 people you spend the most time with." - Jim Rohn

The second piece of valuable advice I got at my first Junto meeting was to start surrounding myself with the right people. My question was, what did that actually mean? Who were the "right" people? Calling anyone a "wrong" person didn't seem fair, but were my friends not the right people? I valued my group of friends and the fun we had together. It seemed ridiculous that I needed to drop my friendships with them if I wanted to move forward in a positive direction.

For the most part my friends were just like me: they were working for the weekends and soaking up all that San Diego had to offer. Sure, they wanted to advance their careers, but who didn't? Some of them would talk about a cool business idea over a few beers, but it was just talk. They were comfortable putting their time in at a desk job from 9-5, and do you know what? I thought I was too. I thought I was doing better than a lot of people and that I was on a great track in life. It took being introduced to a different group of people for me to realize I was far, far off.

I can't overstate the impact it had on me when I walked into that first meeting only to discover that among my peers, I was far behind the learning curve. I felt out of place because I didn't have anything to contribute. At a time like that, all you can do is either retreat or fight your way up. Something inside me knew that being around those people on a weekly basis would be transformative.

Maybe I had nothing to offer yet, but I felt challenged to catch up to the group and show them what I could do. I was blessed to have had the opportunity to attend and to be welcomed into the "tribe". I got to see firsthand the domino effect of life events which were created by surrounding myself with the 'right' people.

Everything you do in life either benefits you or it doesn't. The people you choose to have interactions with, the food you eat, even the shoes you buy. You can take a look at anyone or anything and ask: "Is this choice serving me?" If you ask this question often enough, you'll find your answers may change.

If you were starving and there was nothing else to eat but McDonalds, then eating it serves you well because it provides calories and keeps you alive. If you're trying to get in shape however, that same meal doesn't serve you well at all. This is the way you can ask the question for every action you take in your life.

For me, I had to ask myself if partying until the early hours of the morning was serving me. I found in my answer that at one time, it was. It was an effective way to make friends in college, meet new people, and take full part of college life, but at this stage of my life, what was it serving?

The Right People

Wasting away the weekends then feeling lethargic at work the next week was not a promising pattern. It wasn't that I had to drop my previous friends; I just had to lower the value I placed on partying.

I began creating a new value system and set of priorities for myself. I valued waking up early on Saturday morning to read a book then go for a run; it made me feel focused and alive. The more I felt that way, the less value I put on drinking. I realized I wasn't getting much out of drinking anyway, except a hangover.

On the nights I did go out, I drank less and became unimpressed by my environment. Watching people slurring their words and talking about nonsense seemed like a waste of time. I realized quickly why having a weekly Friday night meeting was so crucial to my success. I had to be the type of person who valued my time enough to invest it around a conference table rather than over more tempting activities. I found that it paid dividends to meet for personal growth at the time most people were raising a glass for happy hour.

Each meeting I found myself feeling lifted to new heights. I went from knowing no entrepreneurs to having deep conversations with eight of them every week. I went from thinking the corporate ladder was the way to go, to looking for opportunities of what work I was going to do for myself one day. Not everyone needs to be an entrepreneur, but I believe a spirit of entrepreneurship should be cultivated in all of us.

That spirit is one of opportunity and growth that can help you in all aspects of your life. The entrepreneur looks to become a better version of him or herself because they know that by doing so, their business will improve. I began to see the positive effects of personal development even though I wasn't an entrepreneur yet. I also started noticing a shift in my mindset.

Find Your Truth

I would be the first one to say that I was a great employee. I did what I was told, and I did it well. I was such a good employee that I would worry about whether my boss thought I was doing a good job. This is where my employee mindset was strong, and my job satisfaction depended on others telling me I was doing a good job. Someone with an entrepreneurial spirit doesn't need that kind of outside reinforcement: they cultivate pride from within.

How can you cultivate this mindset if you find yourself surrounded by its opposite?

CHAPTER 19

The Wrong People

"The Fastest way to get where you want to go is to surround yourselves with people already doing it."- Scott Dinsmore

The influences you let into your life become your subconscious role models. I didn't realize this at the time, but I was being influenced by many things in my environment. From the hard party lifestyle I thought was "cool" to the Lil Wayne songs I listened to, my reality was gradually being shaped.

When you start finding new role models and influences, you will see changes in the person you become. Those changes may not always be welcomed by the people who knew you before. You will face some resistance from people you care about. When you decide to make notable changes in your life, that also means you might be making someone else's life change as well.

In the months following the changes I had been making in my lifestyle, some of my friends got suspicious. They would ask me why I wasn't going out as much, and questioned my new hobbies. Some even took offense, as if the change in my life was a sign I didn't like them. As I mentioned earlier, you don't have to drop all your friends but you'll find that as your values start changing, your friends might start dropping you. It sucks to say that many of my friendships were based on partying, so as I partied less, those relationships naturally came to an end.

A close friend let me in on what other people were saying behind my back. It was evident they couldn't understand and were uncomfortable with the new person I was becoming. Because of this, it became obvious to me who my real friends were and who liked me only if I played a certain role in their life. It was a sobering truth, but ultimately it was for the better.

I was becoming happier and a few of my friends felt betrayed because of the changes I was making. I'm not sure about you, but this doesn't seem like a healthy friendship. A true friend should be happy you're taking steps to improve your life. If they show resistance and want you to be the person you were before, that's a red flag. It's a tough realization, but you have to take inventory of who you let into your life and the roles they play.

This doesn't mean that you should only look to bring people into your life that can help you get where you're going. It's important to have some people who you can support along *their* path, too. Initially, when it came to tangible accomplishments, I was far behind everyone in the Junto group. If it hadn't been for their influence in my life, I wouldn't have been able to progress so quickly.

You have to act as a sort of conduit, getting support from people who are where you want to be, and giving it to others who want to be where you are. There's a natural order of things and if you don't reciprocate the good that comes your

The Wrong People

way, you block meaningful, continual flow. It is said that the easiest way to get what you want is to give it away first: if you can support other people along their path, you just might find more people coming into your life to support you.

Another question to ask when taking account of the influences in your life is: "Is this person supportive?" When you tell someone about a new idea you have, do they have positive words of encouragement or do they try to shoot you down? Some people should be avoided because they often have nothing good to say about anything.

If they couldn't do or achieve something they wanted, they don't know what to tell you other than *you can't either*. They might have good intentions, thinking they're trying to keep you safe from failure. All I can say is that if it's a close family member and you value your relationship with them, try to manage the conversations as best you can. If it's a friend, it may be a sign that you should spend less time with that person.

Ultimately you don't have control over what other people do, but you do have full control over the influences you allow into your life. It's obvious, but it's the awareness of it that makes it so transformative. Growing up, I had no idea how deep of an impact my surroundings had on me. In my current state of awareness I can look back and easily connect the dots.

As I mentioned earlier, each of us has a unique perspective. We live in our own sense of what is "normal", which may be wildly different from our neighbor. Think about what a "normal" week for a homeless person is, compared to a "normal" week for Bill Gates. While this is an extreme comparison, the example helped me see how what was "normal" to me helped shape my life.

In high school, doing drugs like cocaine and ecstasy was taboo, and not something I would ever consider myself doing. It was far from "normal". As I got older and found myself in social circles that included this habit, all of a sudden the behavior became normal. When something becomes normal to you, it doesn't seem that crazy, but it's a good idea to pause and take a moment to think about what you're doing from someone else's perspective: would *they* say that behavior is normal?

If you're hanging out with a bunch of drunken buffoons, chances are you're going to be a drunken buffoon. If you want fulfillment in your life, hang out with people who feel fulfilled. It may seem like beating a dead horse at this point, but it's so crucial that you understand the impact your environment has on your life. It wasn't always "normal" for me to read books and spend time in reflection, but now it's become a part of my life.

Look to cultivate more friendships with people in your life who make you feel good. How many people do you know right now who are encouraging you to follow your dreams, or make an impact on the world? Work to consistently increase that number, and you'll move closer to achieving your goals. By surrounding yourself with people who are actively living their passion, you'll have no choice but to live yours.

How to Find the Right People

Here's an exercise you can do: grab a pen and paper and write down all the people in your life who inspire you to become a better person. You don't have to know all of them personally; they could be anyone who influences you to become the person you want to be.

After you've done this, write down names of people who have the opposite effect on you. Do you have a friend who always wants you to drink all day on the weekends, and makes fun of you if you don't? How about the co-worker who is constantly complaining about the company, but doesn't do anything to change it? What media influences do you let into your life? Do you feel good after watching the news? How about people you follow on social media?

Compare this list and work to increase the positive influences and let go of the negative ones. A great way to increase the positive influences is to find a group like I did. I never realized groups like Junto existed, and maybe you don't either. I encourage you to find a group like this you can meet with. While doing something you're passionate about may seem like a solo endeavor, you can't do it alone. You will need the support of people who understand the journey and who believe in you. As I'll discuss in the next chapter, it's a good practice to get out of your comfort zone and try something new.

CHAPTER 20

The Push

"If you put yourself in a position where you have to stretch outside your comfort zone, then you are forced to expand your consciousness." - Les Brown

What I liked most about making changes in my life was that I was continually pushing my comfort zone. When Friday came along, I was no longer excited about the weekend ahead: instead, I had a nervous anticipation for the Friday night meetings. Even after a month of being part of the group, I would have small panic attacks while waiting for my turn to speak. I was petrified, but I got immediate feedback which showed me how transformative pushing my comfort zone could be.

The discomfort I felt matched the level of growth I was experiencing: it seemed to be in direct correlation. The more times I put myself outside my comfort zone, the more alive I felt, and the more good things seemed to happen.

Find Your Truth

This new mentality spilled over into every aspect of my life. I became more determined to turn my life around. For example, I had always lifted weights in the gym, but now I lifted harder. I was always courteous to people at work, but now I was taking a real interest in others' lives and being more generous with my time. I had always eaten healthy food, but now I was making an effort to eat more whole foods.

Pushing my comfort zone basically amplified the good that was already in my life, and brought with it a bounty of new benefits as well. When it came to making powerful changes, what shot directly to the forefront was my desire to move up in my company. As I mentioned earlier, I managed account receivables and made collection calls to our customers as a "Credit Analyst." I liked my boss, but I just couldn't see myself becoming a "Credit Manager" in 10 years.

I felt a desire to do something bigger and more meaningful for the company. I knew that I had let myself get too comfortable with the routine of my job, and I was slowly gaining the confidence to do something about it. I started looking for opportunities, a prime example of how people can proactively change their environment. I was surrounded by entrepreneurs and if I wanted to really fit in with the group, I felt a need to grow.

I didn't see myself leaving the company and starting a business just yet, so I channeled my energy into getting promoted instead. I didn't know what position I wanted, but I felt called to do marketing, for the sole reason that it would allow me to do something creative. I had a strong desire to put my own personal stamp on moving the company forward.

I kept a piece of paper on my nightstand that read, "I will get a job in marketing." My mind was set on this outcome, and I found insights coming to me on how to make that happen.

The Push

This was my first real-life experience using the power of my mind to "manifest" something I wanted.

One of the ideas that emerged from a conversation was to simply tell the CEO about my interest in advancing within the company. At first, this idea seemed unimaginable. Who was I to go up to the head of the company and tell him what I wanted? The man was far above my pay grade. I pondered this limiting belief until I thought about what the other side of the equation might look like: what would happen if I actually did it?

I imagined myself walking up to the CEO, saying, "Dave, this is what I want, and this is what I can do." Was it crazy? I put myself in the CEO's shoes. If I were him, wouldn't I want my employees to be ambitious, hoping to make a contribution to the company? Of course I would. Once I realized this, I let my imagination run wild with what the possible outcomes could be. I took a sheet of paper and started to write out some of the things I would say. Thinking about it made me nervous and uncomfortable: that's how I knew this idea was worth further exploration.

I've found that when dealing with things that are uncomfortable, it's best to ask yourself the question I did: what possibilities are on the other side? Creating experiences outside your comfort zone can be good when what lies beyond your discomfort is something that excites you. Stabbing yourself in the leg with a fork would be uncomfortable, but it doesn't hold a promising future. On the other hand, taking action to conquer a long-existing fear does.

Pushing your comfort zone is necessary because it will show a side of yourself you never knew existed. Being uncomfortable is key to growth and evolution. It's up to you to put that evolutionary pressure on yourself because no one else is going to do it for you.

CHAPTER 21

The Defining Moment

"There came a time when the risk to remain tight in the bud was more painful than the risk it took to blossom." – Anaïs Nin

I figured that my talk with the CEO would happen at some point far into the future; I had no idea how soon the chance to have this talk would present itself. That's what happens when you set your mind to something; if it's in line with your actions, things can happen much faster than you would have ever imagined.

The talk I visualized with the CEO is a great example. The day started out as a typical one. I got into the office around 7:00 AM and booted my computer up for the day's work ahead. As I grabbed a cup of coffee and settled back at my desk, I noticed the CEO walking through the room and upstairs to his office. It was typical of him to make himself visible to his employees, and I respected the fact that he went out of his way to do this.

The only thing different about this particular day was that he was two hours early.

At this moment a light came on in my head. I knew that he would be the only one upstairs at this time of day, which would be the perfect opportunity to talk to him. As that initial thought surfaced, I shot it right back down with a laugh. I thought this moment would be months down the road, and I was in no position to act now.

I tried brushing the idea aside and got back to my work, but what started out as a whisper got louder, and my heart jumped at the thought of what the "other side" of this fear and doubt could bring. The other side looked to me like a new level of triumph. The thought persisted until it prevented me from being able to focus on my work.

With my mind racing, I got out of my chair and walked out the door into our warehouse, finding a private space to see if I could psych myself up. I paced back and forth, slowed my breath down and gave myself a few words of encouragement.

"Slow down Lou; you can do this."

I thought I was ready.

I walked back through the doors and stood below the stairwell that led to his office. Like someone uncertain about fully walking into a dark room, I took two cautious steps up the stairs, only to pause and retreat. I wasn't quite ready yet.

I walked down to my cubicle to grab a cup of water and headed back out to the warehouse to restart the process. I gulped down the water and began taking slow, deep breaths. I used my imagination to breathe in the courage I needed, and breathe out the fear that was causing my hesitation. I ran through another affirmation.

The Defining Moment

"Focus, you got this."

I headed back to the stairwell, taking one last calming breath, and then began my ascent. This time as I stood at the step where I last retreated, I said to myself: "On this next step, there's no turning back. You're fully committed."

I took that next step, and up I went. I moved with conviction up the stairs and towards the CEO's office.

What happened after I took that deciding step had somewhat a life of its own. It seemed my words and body language just happened without effort: later I realized I had just let myself be completely in the moment, speaking my truth.

I knocked on his door and poked my head in. "Dave, you got a minute?" I could tell he was surprised, yet curious. I stepped inside and with confidence I said, "I can be the best Credit Analyst this company has ever seen, but I know in my heart I have much more to offer."

He encouraged me to take a seat and what happened next was a 20-minute conversation about my personal life and career aspirations. He told me there wasn't a position available now, but he would definitely keep me in mind for the future. As I left, he told me he wished he had 160 employees just like me.

As I walked out of his office, I felt like a David who just beaten Goliath. I didn't even care if I was getting a new position or not. I knew this was a defining moment I could always look back on. It was a lesson for me about what happens when I fully commit.

When I headed back downstairs, I could barely sit still at my desk. I was as high as a kite on a feeling I never knew I could experience. It was a kind of ecstasy I had never felt before; like floating on a cloud. In the state I was in now, I couldn't focus at all on my work.

Find Your Truth

My thoughts turned to an errand I had to run at the DMV. I went into my manager's office and told him about my talk with the CEO and to ask if I could take off work early. He knew about my aspirations so he was excited for me, and told me it was fine to leave. As I left the office I thought, "Well, there will never, in the history of the DMV, be a happier person standing in line than I am right now."

So there I was, standing in line at the DMV. I was blasting Jay-Z and Kanye West's "Who Gon' Stop Me" through my earbuds, smiling from ear to ear, and not so silently singing the words under my breath. I'm sure the people around me were either questioning my sanity or sobriety.

They wouldn't have been far off. I was high, but the feeling wasn't from a pill, drink or powder. It was something you have to work hard for, a feeling that comes from within. I stood in that line for three hours in complete bliss, waiting to get my new drivers license.

The date was July 10th, so I have since referred to this day's event as my "7/10" moment. I celebrate it as a time when I felt the fear, but proceeded anyway. To this day I can still feel the energy pulse through my body, thinking about how incredible that feeling was.

This served as another example of what happens when I step outside my comfort zone. It was positive reinforcement that this newfound zest for life could be multiplied by steps I take into the unknown. Within just a few weeks of being introduced to the new concepts I had been learning in my weekly meetings, I had grabbed the baton and started running.

I couldn't wait to go to our meeting that Friday and tell everyone about my personal breakthrough and what had happened. It was the first time I wasn't nervous; I had a sense of pride that I had done something worth talking about, and it felt

The Defining Moment

like I was finally able to make a legitimate contribution to the group.

I used my "7/10" moment as a springboard to continue my newfound personal growth. If this was just the beginning, how much farther could I go? What else was out there that I hadn't yet experienced? I made a commitment to myself that the natural high I felt after leaving the CEO's office was something I want to continually feel for the rest of my life. I knew I wanted to do more to keep that feeling.

In the months to come, I would learn more about that feeling and the true bliss that is our natural birthright. To say that I continued along this path of life-expansion would be a big understatement.

CHAPTER 22

The Growth

"Without continual growth and progress, such words as improvement, achievement, and success have no meaning."-Benjamin Franklin

After my "7/10" experience, I felt like I had conquered the world and could do anything I set my mind to. I was unstoppable with my new way of life, and my mind continued to be programmed to see opportunities around me. I was finally taking control of my life instead of getting blown wherever the wind took me. I was obsessed with personal development, and the person I was becoming.

I was partying less and *living* more. It was through this that I learned a key universal truth: as you evolve into a better version of yourself, you begin to have a positive impact on those around you. It's through this impact that you benefit too, because it comes back to you in so many ways.

My mindset shifted from "what can I get?" to "what can I give?" I would go to work excited about something new I'd been learning and I'd feel compelled to share it with my co-workers. They were seeing a new, motivated and ambitious Lou which made them want to better themselves too. I was paying more attention to what they were going through than I had before, and offering whatever help I could. I was also receiving much more in return than I could have imagined.

I realized that everything wasn't just all about me. In the end it wouldn't matter what I did if I forgot about the importance of relationships, or just tried to get ahead in spite of (or because of) competition. My effort to move forward wasn't about comparison at all. It was about personal and communal growth, which included bringing others along with me.

My participation in our Friday night mastermind group showed me the power of group effort, and I felt obligated to continue the domino effect. For example, I sought to be the reason someone else had a good day. I brought good will to each situation and began taking more of a genuine interest in other people. It wasn't forced because it felt natural to share this new gift I had been given. I was genuinely and wholeheartedly inspired.

I aspired to make my life better and to use my time wisely. Rather than wasting five hours watching television, I could conquer my fears, like talking to my company's CEO about my ambitions. I also wanted to help anyone who crossed my path; I was inspired to inspire.

It felt great when someone approached me, saying their life had improved because of something I said or did. There was no feeling like it. I felt like I was contributing to something bigger than myself, and that inspired me to keep pushing things to the next level.

The more inspired I got, the happier I became. That happiness was multiplied any time I got feedback that I had a positive impact on someone else's life. I believe one of the cures to

The Growth

feeling low is to make someone else feel high. Try giving away whatever it is you want to receive, and it could come back to you fourfold.

Once I started shifting my life towards service and personal growth, ideas came to my mind, and I acted on them. I learned that I could change anything I wanted in my life, no matter what it was. Making change starts with making a choice. When you make a decision to change something you don't like, you're taking control of your destiny.

We were born with free will and it's our birthright to make choices and control our reality. If you ever think you "don't have a choice" you've submitted to a lower version of yourself and basically let go of your responsibility. At this level, you're simply reacting to situations and leaving control of your life up to someone or something else.

The sad reality is most people go through life like this. They blame their circumstances on their parents, their kids, their lack of resources, or anything that can get them off the hook. They blame others so they don't have to take responsibility for the way their life is turning out.

I saw some of this in my own life before I learned this principle. Like most people in their jobs, I felt like I was underpaid. I also constantly felt like I wasn't being treated fairly and that others were always better off than I was.

I had this one particular friend who always seemed to have good things happen in his life. Once he told me he got a raise at work and instead of being happy for him, I was jealous. I thought, "Why do good things always happen to him and not me? Why is he the lucky one and I always get dealt the bad hand?" Instead of taking charge of my circumstances, I played the victim.

Once I woke up and realized how detrimental that mindset was, I took control of my life. Anything I was experiencing that wasn't my ideal, I looked for ways to change it. Sometimes it was an easy choice like watching less TV; other times it was really difficult.

The hardest thing I had to do was take a look at my current relationship with Kelly and bring to the surface something I'd been thinking about for awhile. Once I stepped up to face it, the transformation in my life grew exponentially. When I made the decision to take full control of every single aspect of my life, my life became better and better.

To quote Napoleon Hill again, "Be definite in everything you do and never leave unfinished thoughts in the mind. Form the habit of reaching definite decisions on all subjects." The hardest decisions often yield the biggest results. Tough decisions can also contain a fear of the unknown, what might happen, or where that decision will take you.

To experience your own transformation, you have to become someone who makes decisions.

CHAPTER 23

The Space

"The great thing in this world is not so much where you stand, as in what direction you are moving." – Oliver Wendell Holmes

Have you ever been in a situation where you felt trapped? For example, maybe you're in a job where you feel stuck. You know something isn't what you want, or where you want to be. You dream all the time about leaving and how life would look if you were in a different situation. Every day you walk into work feeling this, but you do nothing. Why?

Why do you live with the gut feeling that something needs to change? Why do you wake up every day doing something that's not in alignment with who you really are? The simple answer is you're scared. But you reason away your fear by saying you don't have a choice.

You say you have bills to pay, a family to feed, a life to live. You say, "I can't make a change now; how would I survive?" You don't know if you would have it in you to leave the job and be forced figure things out. You leave yourself no out.

You're "trapped". You've dug this hole and now you have to live in it. You have no other choice, right? Wrong.

I know this feeling well, although it wasn't with my job. I felt trapped in my relationship with Kelly. Kelly and I had moved into the 3-bedroom apartment we shared with two of my male friends. Living with my girlfriend and friends seemed like a great idea, and for a while, it was. When Kelly had to stay in on the weekends to study, I had a group of friends I could go out with.

The apartment as a whole had enough room for all four of us, with a nice patio that expanded our space. It was in a beautiful location just seven blocks from the beach and walking distance to the picturesque San Diego bay front.

During the initial move-in, we were giddy with excitement about everything that was happening: Kelly was moving across the country to be with me, and I was moving into my first real apartment after college life. Before moving there, I had been subletting a room in an older lady's apartment, so I didn't really feel like the place was my own. This new place was.

It might not have been the ideal situation for a couple to live with other people, especially two of us just out of college, but we made it work. Kelly and I missed out on some fun "couple" activities like quiet dinners at home or movie nights in the living room, but I was okay with that. What I wasn't okay with was a growing awareness inside of me that I was feeling trapped.

I started to grow jealous of the life my roommates had. They were single guys living in a beach town with a great selection of good-looking women. When we went out together, I'd see them hitting on girls without a care in the world, and there was some part of me that missed that.

The Space

I remembered what it felt like in college, when the nights held endless opportunities, and the exciting thought of the unknown woman I might find myself in bed with. It kept the nights fresh and engaging. Having Kelly move across country so we could live together felt like a big commitment and I found myself longing for freedom.

What also played into this uncomfortable feeling was my jealous nature. I had always been a man with a laundry list of insecurities. This went back to my desire to fit in with the crowd, and to be the coolest guy in the group. When I went out with Kelly, I got annoyed at every guy who looked at her or tried striking up a conversation with her. I know many insecure men in relationships who can easily relate to this.

I felt like the encroaching guy was threatening my manhood, and I often got offended. I couldn't enjoy nights out like this, especially while drinking. The alcohol only seemed to exaggerate my jealousy and feelings of being trapped. With the effects of alcohol, I'd become that drunk, angry boyfriend: the kind of person I couldn't stand.

I stopped looking forward to the weekends. Everything seemed dull and boring compared to the excitement of college parties. Now I was just a guy going to a job he thought was expected of him, living with his girlfriend, reminiscing on how "good" things were back in college.

The worst part about this was that I thought I had no way out. Kelly left everything she knew to move across the country to live with me. I couldn't tell her how I was feeling, and just leave her alone. Just like someone could be feeling with a job or other commitment, I felt trapped in this relationship.

I felt like I had gotten myself into this situation and there was nothing I could do about it. I just had to make the best of it and push this suffocating feeling back down. Doing this made me feel even more depressed, though. The only thing that gave me relief from this feeling I had inside was taking ecstasy. It gave me a fleeting feeling of happiness. It was my escape from being in the hole I had dug for myself. That happiness morphed into depression because of the effects of the drug, but I could live with that.

Deep down I was aching for excitement. I couldn't go out and hit on a bunch of girls, so the drugs were my only way to get this feeling. On nights I didn't have drugs available, I would go into my own mental "cave". Drinking made me feel worse, so I would often just go home early from bars and head straight to bed. The weekends started to come and go, feeling like dull relief from a dull work week.

This was the life I created, and mine to deal with. There were no options to get out: I was stuck. Stuck that is, until I found the Junto group. It was then that I began to reprogram my thinking and I realized there was always a way out of a particular life circumstances you find yourself in, or something you don't want. You always have choices.

After getting positive results from facing uncomfortable situations and coming out ahead, I started to entertain the notion of facing the most uncomfortable situation of all: bringing my feelings up to Kelly.

I was petrified of breaking her heart, and I also felt like it was going to be an ordeal to begin the process of moving out and finding another place to live. The whole thing seemed overwhelming, but it didn't change how I felt. I knew the right thing to do; I had just been too scared to do it.

I looked at all the fear that was staring me in the face and decided to take just one step forward. It wasn't fair to Kelly for me to withhold how I had been feeling. I began this daunting ordeal by bringing it up in conversation one night in early August 2014, a month after my "7/10" moment.

The Space

This was truly the biggest fear I had faced yet. Unlike the first two uncomfortable situations, this involved someone else's life. As I sat with Kelly in our bedroom and tried to talk about my feelings, I had a lot of inner resistance. Similar to my first steps up the stairs to my CEO's office, I hesitated. I started talking, but danced around what I really wanted to say. I couldn't find the courage to say it, but by the way I was acting, she started to get the idea.

I finally blurted out, "something's not working." After an initial pause from Kelly, the response that followed shocked me. She wasn't heartbroken, but appreciative that we were finally having this conversation. Kelly said she could sense something was up with me for awhile. She admitted she was feeling some of the same things. We talked for a few hours about everything, and ended up with much more clarity about our relationship.

We decided we should spend time apart for a while. We didn't know what that would look like, but it felt great to come to a mutual understanding. All the anxiety that had been building up inside of me had been released. All the fear I had made up in my mind was just that, made up. I was shown once again what happens when you face a fear head on. It always seems more daunting than it is, and on the other side lies the treasure.

The logistics of moving out of our apartment still had to be handled and a lot of people who were going to be surprised by the news, but we had taken the first step. Kelly and I lived together for more than a month after that before finally parting ways. What's crazy is that our relationship was better in that month than it had been the past year.

I learned something valuable about relationships during that time. Radical honesty may be hard, but it's the easiest way to help things go more smoothly. If you have a feeling inside, it doesn't do any good to keep it in. It takes a real man or woman to express their true feelings. This can be rare because we've been conditioned to do the opposite.

When you express how you feel, there's no longer anything to hide, nothing to clutter up your mind and play with your emotions. Instead, you feel a sense of calm. It's your soul saying you've done the best thing, and your reward is peace of mind. A lot of discontent and dis"ease" later in life is often brought about by holding emotions in for so long. The energy has to move somewhere: let it out.

I continued to reap the benefits of facing challenges that scared or overwhelmed me. I was building up a unique muscle that I would need to be successful; not success in monetary terms (although that comes too with personal growth), but success as a human being. I was gradually becoming a success by being courageous and honest. With every step I took into the unknown, my moral compass strengthened: I became clear about who I was and what I wanted from life. My intuition kept leading me into new, unfamiliar territory. The more I trusted it and acted on it, the more I grew.

After breaking up with Kelly I was free to jump into the next chapter of my life. It was a chapter that was completely unknown, and that was what excited me the most. I felt in control of my life, and I could feel things transforming around me.

I knew that fortune favors the bold. My new journey was happening fast, and I was buckled up and ready for the ride.

CHAPTER 24

The Journal

"There are only two mistakes one can make along the road to truth; not going all the way, and not starting." – The Buddha

After my breakup with Kelly, I moved into a one-bedroom apartment about 20 minutes from the beach, to a San Diego community called North Park. Similar to Brooklyn, it had an urban hipster vibe. It was a part of the city I was completely unfamiliar with, and I think that's what interested me about it. It was a time in my life I was exploring new things, and a new environment seemed fitting.

I was happy to have my own space where I could enjoy peace and quiet. Living in a beach house with rowdy 23 year olds didn't allow for many relaxing weekends. On my last night before moving, I came home from a great Junto meeting hoping to get some sleep to start moving my stuff early the next morning, but I walked into a huge party my roommates were having at our place. The raising of shot glasses and blasting techno music had never annoyed me so much as it did on that particular night. It was a sign that read, "It's time to get the F--k out of here." I was so ready for the morning to come so I could begin my move.

Although the freedom to meet other women was part of my initial reason for breaking up with Kelly, I knew that I really needed some time to be alone. So many incredible things were happening and I felt this push towards something bigger. I wanted a deeper level of self-exploration so I needed space to grow and discover. This was an opportunity to spend my time reading, reflecting, and thanks to the best gift I'd ever received...writing.

Just prior to moving, a friend had gifted me a custom designed journal. The beauty of it was he didn't know I had been thinking about starting a journal. The topic of keeping a journal had been coming up frequently in recent discussions, and how important it was. At first the idea that grown men would write down their feelings seemed laughable to me; I thought something like that was only for high school girls. At the time, I wasn't aware that some of the most successful people in the world kept a journal.

In any case, it was on my radar to start one but I hadn't yet pulled the trigger. As the Universe always does, it gives you what you need when the time is right. Alone with my space to sit and write, the time had come for me to start this second most transformational practice of my life: writing.

If all you take away from this book is to consider this activity too, and just write one sentence of your thoughts down, it would be worth your time. You don't have to like writing or consider yourself a good writer to enjoy journaling or receive its benefits. You also don't need a lot of time, and you don't need a long list of things to write about.

The Journal

Julia Cameron wrote many books about creativity. She explains the benefits of journal-writing, or as she calls her practice, "Morning Pages" and writes "Little by little what we have to say and who we have to say it to will become clear to us. The truth, the whole truth is a gradual process." She also encourages beginners to have compassion for their writing.

I didn't know what I would be in for when I started to journal, but there were some basic guidelines I followed that led to great results. I list them here to give you a better idea of how you can start journaling if you're new at it.

Don't Put Pressure on Yourself

I once asked a friend if she kept a journal. Her response was, "I don't have that much self-discipline." I don't know what's more surprising - that she thought journaling had to have strict rules, or that she believed I had a lot of self-discipline.

It saddened me to hear her response because maybe that's how most people feel about it. They think a journal has to be a day-by-day account that includes details like what they had for dinner or other trivial specifics from their day. This is far from the case.

Especially when starting out, you shouldn't put any pressure on how often you write or what you write about. You're starting this practice to benefit yourself, not self imposing an hour's worth of work each day.

Your journal is a place to get your thoughts and ideas on paper, and you're allowed to make this practice whatever you want it be. With this mentality, I got started and wasn't strict about how much I wrote. Some days I wrote a few pages and other days I just wrote a sentence. If I was feeling tired I would just write a short entry, for example:

9/22/14

"I'm stuck between whether I want to read or write. I just got too tired to continue writing, lol"

That's a journal entry!

Write at Least a Word Every Other Day When You Start

This is somewhat in contradiction to my first point, but if you're someone who has a resistance to writing, this may be a good place to start. Writing is a practice that you get better at the more you do it. Just getting one word down that describes how you felt that day can be a step in the right direction.

What you write about could be something you want to work on, such as patience for example. Date your page in the morning and write down "patience." Of course you could take it a step further and write a whole sentence, but you don't have to. What's important is that you start getting into a habit of opening your journal and making an entry.

Again, don't be strict with yourself. Start with easily attainable goals and work your way up. If you can't do one word a day, do one word a week and go from there. What happens is that when you go to write your word, you'll trick yourself into writing more. Soon, you may lose yourself in writing page after page.

Don't Hide What You're Feeling

When people don't write how they truly feel they're either afraid to admit it or worried about what others might think. Right off the bat one of these possibilities can't be you, because your journal is for no one's eyes but yours. When you're walking down the street, the people around you can't hear your

The Journal

thoughts, and guess what? They're not reading your journal either.

The point of journaling is to get all your rambling thoughts out of your mind and onto paper. Journaling is a therapeutic practice. If you don't write how you truly feel, you are doing yourself a disservice.

You might resist writing down a thought because doing so makes it more real. These are the thoughts and ideas to take a closer look at. The more scared you are to write something, the more it should come out. It doesn't do you any good to brush it off to the side and pretend it doesn't exist. Journaling helps to unwind unpleasant emotions before they cause problems.

When you acknowledge something you can't just sweep under the rug, you're taking responsibility for it. It's only then that you can work through what you're scared of. Take full advantage of your journal by writing your truth. You owe it to yourself.

Write About Where You See Yourself

Whether it be daydreaming, wishful thinking, or goal setting, write about how you would like to see yourself months or years down the road. At some point in our lives we forget that awesome things can actually happen to us. We write our dreams off, and head towards paths that have already been laid out.

Use your journal as a place to dream big again. No one is there to judge you, so don't feel like you have to be modest. Write about the dream house on the ocean you see yourself and a wonderful partner or spouse living in. Write about the promotion you know you're going to get. Write about how awesome your life is, and will be.

Be creative. The bigger the dream, the better. Write often, and write powerfully. Don't hold back and don't be afraid to let it all out. The more you write about your ideal life, the more you train your mind to find ways to make it happen.

The reasons people don't get what they want:

1. They don't know what they want
2. They don't ask

Journaling helps you with both. It gives you a medium to explore inside your head and your heart to find what gives you joy. Then, if you have an idea, don't be afraid to ask. How else do you think you can get it?

From the many books on self-development I've read, this habit of writing down what you want is encouraged in all of them. This helps you to program your sub-conscious mind.

I wrote a lot in my journal about finding my real purpose and becoming the best version of myself. With that mindset, I've narrowed my focus to activities that take me closer to that goal. I also wrote about writing a book one day, which is what you're reading.

Write About What You're Grateful for

"Acknowledging the good that you already have in your life is the foundation for all abundance." -Eckhart Tolle

If you can't think of what to write, there are two words that always make a great entry: "Thank you." If you were able to purchase this book and you can read it, you already have so

The Journal

much to be grateful for. Gratitude may seem obvious and cliché, but if you really dig down deep with it, it can change your life.

We all have problems and discontent in our lives, but it does no good to focus on them. Gratitude forces you to focus on the good things in your life rather than complaining about the bad. When you focus on the good, you train your mind to find the positive in every situation throughout the day.

When I started journaling, I wrote three things I was grateful for each morning. There's nothing wrong with writing about things like family, finances, and a roof over your head. If more people were to feel truly grateful about these, there would be fewer people walking around like zombies.

As you continue this practice of gratitude, you may find yourself at a loss for things to write down. It doesn't need to be something profound you're grateful for every time. Look back to the previous day and pick out obvious but overlooked things. I'm a runner, so there are many times I'm grateful that I have the use of my legs and I'm able to do this activity that I love so much.

Maybe try scanning yourself from head to toe and be grateful for something. Be grateful you're able to breathe, sleep, or even use the bathroom on your own. You might laugh, but there are people who don't have these things. Be grateful for the paved streets you drive on, a grocery store you can go to, or that you have food to eat. It really is the small things in life we often take for granted, until disaster strikes.

Bathe your life in gratitude! The more you bring gratitude into your life, the more life you feel like living. Practicing gratitude each morning inspired me to write a poem that I repeat to myself each day.

Better Today
I will be better today than I was yesterday.
I will be stronger today than I was yesterday.
I will learn more today than I knew yesterday.
But most important, I am grateful for today,
For today is an opportunity.
Today is a gift.
Today is the most important day of my life.

Don't live every day like it's the last; live it like it's the most important day, because it is. There's nothing in your life more important than the present moment. It's an opportunity that we are all blessed to have. Writing what you're grateful for each day grounds you to the present moment and allows you to appreciate where you are instead of focusing so much on the future or thinking about the past.

Life is here and now, and it's a blessing. The more you approach it from this perspective, the more good life can have in store for you. Make your gratitude practice a sacred time. See if you can catch yourself during the day feeling grateful in any given moment. Look to capture these moments more often so you can have more to write about later. It's a beautiful upward spiral.

CHAPTER 25

The Proof of Transformation

Here's one last point about journaling, which can be the most transformational.

Look Back Through Your Journal at Least Once a Month

What never fails to give me chills is when I read something I wrote and it seems like someone else wrote it. It could be something I foresaw that actually happened, or I wrote something more profound than what I'd think would come from my own pen. When you're reading something you wrote a week or a month ago, there's a certain detachment you have from the writing. It's not *you* you're reading about; it's a previous version of you. You may also see yourself as naïve, and other times you could surprise yourself.

Journaling is the best way for you to reflect on your progress; it's written proof of your transformation. It takes account of all the magic you've been creating which began with your thoughts. We often don't realize how much we've grown until we are reminded about something from our past. We often forget the seeds we planted that have since become flowers. Journaling is really history in the making.

The more you look back on your journal entries, the more shocked you might be when you see the evolution of your life unfold. If you're searching for your life purpose for example, reading back through your journal could give you hints as to what that might be. You might see patterns in what you wrote about and what you're attracted to. When you let your thoughts flow, the power of your subconscious mind comes out more freely. You can use this to your benefit when you look back at what you wrote.

When I read about the seeds of my new ways of thinking, I feel humbled to have started on my journey to inspire others. Here are some of my early entries that give me chills when I read them:

8/21/14

"...Thinking has never felt so good...To feel endless possibilities is the way all humans should feel. It would change the world more than it already has."

9/3/14

"...I started having anxiety about things coming up in my life and how much change is happening. All I can do from this point on is take each moment as it comes and prepare the best I can for it. It's time now to get back on track, stay focused and committed, then leave the rest to faith."

The Proof of Transformation

9/6/14

"...I really can't handle pointless conversations anymore. I feel like it's a waste of time. Makes me realize why I used to get drunk just to have a good time."

9/15/14

"...My friend told me about his trip to Vegas to go clubbing. I question if it is on par with the life I truly want to lead. I think I'll know when I'm ready..."

9/26/14

"...I had a slight moment of un-comfortableness. The change is starting to set in and I have been preparing to go through this. The complete aloneness can for sure be scary, but I truly know deep down in my heart it's what I need right now. It will help me in this journey I've already been on with finding myself."

I could go on and on sharing excerpts from my journal that give insight into my own transformative journey. It's as if when I was writing, the realizations came to me from another place. I was basically documenting the evolution that was taking place from a higher, wiser and detached perspective.

My journaling is the reason I was able to write this book. If I hadn't started some sort of writing practice, I would never have been able to persist each day to make this dream a reality. That is what you're reading right now: my dream. A dream that started as a thought and made its way to become a physical reality. Journaling can play a large part in making your dreams happen too, whatever they might be.

The benefits for journaling reach far beyond the act of writing. Your journal is your personal account of life and of you. Years down the road, you'll leave an invaluable gift to your family, giving them a connection to you that might not exist any other way. Imagine if you could read about your great-grandfather's life; how he lived, his way of thinking, his timeless wisdom. He wouldn't be some far-off relative anymore. Instead you'd have a view into his soul. You'd have a relationship with him that couldn't have existed otherwise.

Throughout the rest of the book, I will include excerpts to drive home how significant a role journaling played in my transformation. Without a place to put down my thoughts and list out my goals, I wouldn't have gotten to the place I wanted to be. If this is the first time you're hearing something about journaling, there's a reason. I encourage you to start a journal now. If this is the 5th time you've heard something like this recommended and you haven't started it yet, what are you waiting for?

CHAPTER 26

The Lunch

If there's one theme I keep emphasizing, it's that I had to keep pushing my boundaries to reach new levels of fulfillment. It's as if after I spring-boarded into a new way of life, I couldn't stop jumping. Like a sponge, I soaked up all the knowledge that came my way and put it into practice. My confidence increased with every step I took.

If you're someone looking to advance in your career or climb the corporate ladder, follow this next section closely. You can also apply the same principles to your efforts with other groups or organizations you may be involved with. As I mentioned earlier, I had set the intention that I was going to move into a marketing position in my company. I didn't know how that was going to happen at the time, but I made a commitment that it would be my focus.

With this new content going into my brain, flashes of inspiration came to me about how to make that happen, including things like walking into my CEO's office. Breaking through the clutter in a company is relatively easy; just look at the default settings everyone operates on. If your company is anything like mine was, people mostly keep to themselves. The only interactions throughout the day are with the co-working cliques they might have formed.

Most people are afraid to stand out from the crowd so they generally keep quiet at their desk. They show up, get their work done, go home, and repeat the same thing every day until the weekend comes. There's a mixture of birthday and holiday parties or other office activities sprinkled in, but for the most part it's a standard routine. If you want to stand out in your company or organization it's simple: do something different.

Ask your boss for what you want, talk to new people, and make it a point to change the office culture. Instead of hoping for things to change, *be* the change. If you take on this role, you can progress quickly. Most people remain stagnant or they're slowly losing steam. If you're one of the few who's on the upward trend, the right people will take notice.

After reading the book *Never Eat Alone* by Keith Ferrazi, I was infused with a whole new idea of what it means to connect with people. It's our nature to want to feel a bond with other human beings. The more you're able to create this bond, the more people will like being around you. This makes everyone happier. The happier other people are when they are around you, the more they spread that positivity to others. You can be the ambassador of a new culture and it won't go unnoticed.

If you can't think of what to do, you could try doing exactly what I did. Sitting at work one morning, I received a text from Kelly. We were separated at the time, but we continued to stay close friends. The text from her read simply, "Do something you've never done before." I put my phone in my pocket and leaned back in my chair, contemplating the random but intriguing message. What could I do at work today that I'd never done before?

The Lunch

I thought about a book I had been reading; Seth Godin's *Poke the Box*. In the book Seth writes about an example of when he started at a new company and did something out of the norm. During his first week he called a lunch with a bunch of executives. His boss didn't like this much, but it got his name on the map, and connections were made.

I thought about doing something similar in my company. With Seth Godin's story and Keith Ferrazzi's mantra of "Never Eat Alone," I decided to put myself out there in a big way. I began crafting an email to my entire company inviting them all to go out to lunch with me. Not all at once, but 1:1. I challenged my coworkers to get out of their comfort zone and set up this lunch with me. I reasoned that it would benefit our corporate culture and help encourage the feeling that we were all working towards one common goal.

Here is the email I wrote, edited to protect privacy. As you read through it, think about how this might go over at your company:

Hello Everyone!
Do you eat lunch with the same people every day? Or maybe just at your desk by yourself? Would it make you uncomfortable going to lunch with someone you don't know, or have never really had a conversation with? ... Good.

Like many of you, I am the first one to answer yes to all these questions. As individuals we become comfortable with the same routine every day. The problem with this is nothing can grow in our comfort zone. It's when we take a step out, meet new people, see different viewpoints, and really learn from one another that we will grow as individuals, and ultimately a company. What better way to do this than changing up a small part of our day to have a conversation with someone you don't know all that well? We all have to eat, why waste that time at our desks alone checking Facebook? (I've never done that)

Take a second to read over our COMPANY VALUES, especially "Entrepreneurial Collaboration." Wouldn't this be a great exercise to improve the transparency between departments, and increase the sense that we are all working towards one ultimate goal?

So here is my challenge to all of you...

If you're someone who takes immediate interest in this, click REPLY and let's set up a lunch.

If you're someone who is hesitant, and feels uncomfortable with the thought, PLEASE JUST CLICK REPLY and let's set up a lunch.

If you're someone who would rather take a golf club swing to the head than even consider this, YOU REALLY SHOULD JUST CLICK REPLY and let's set up a lunch.

My hope is that you won't just have lunch with me, but reach out to other people you wouldn't normally consider. I truly think it will have a big impact in strengthening the company culture.

Looking forward to getting to know you all better!

Cheers,
Lou

The Lunch

This email I sent opened up a new world for me. While not everyone set up a lunch to meet with me, I did succeed in making an impression. I got to interact with people I had never talked with before and I made myself known as someone who takes the initiative. It took people by surprise, and that's exactly how to stand out: do something unexpected and you'll be remembered for it.

There are so many opportunities to do this within a company. Whether you're a janitor or executive, you have the opportunity to set yourself apart. Take action when the right time presents itself and head towards that uncomfortable space. Let your intuition be your guide, leading you to act.

Some ideas to start on a smaller scale include sending a motivational quote via email to the people in your department. Pick one person who the quote reminded you of. Making people feel special (not in a manipulative way, but sincerely) by showing your appreciation goes a long way.

Trust me, I know what you're thinking. "If I send an inspirational quote out to my department some of them will think it's weird." You know what, maybe they will! WHO CARES? The people who are making fun of you will be in the same place 5 years from now while you're in upper management or better yet, running your 7-figure business from somewhere across the world. Are you still concerned about people thinking it's weird?

CHAPTER 27

The Successful

A huge positive that came out of my "Lunch with Lou" experiment was the chance to have lunch with my CEO. I had already pitched to him what I wanted, but now I had the opportunity to discuss it in more depth. I couldn't wait to learn from him too, putting to use some of the things that made him so successful. I saw it as my big opportunity to make the strongest connection yet.

I had been learning so much about how to transform my life and I felt like our lunch would be like a coaching session on steroids. I thought for sure the CEO's knowledge would surpass that of many people I'd met the past few months.

As the lunch came and went, I couldn't help but come away surprised. During the time we spoke, I didn't feel much like the mentee employee learning from the mentor CEO. He definitely had more business knowledge and experience but during our conversation, I felt like I connected with him as an equal. I was able to stimulate a thoughtful conversation, sharing different topics and viewpoints.

The lunch went well and a connection was made but I didn't feel like I gained the key to the Universe that I had been expecting. There was one thing he said that stuck with me long after that lunch, though. As he was eating his apricot salad, I asked him what he believed to be his recipe to having such a successful career. With my mental notepad on full alert, I eagerly anticipated his response. My anticipation came to a full stop when he responded: "I wouldn't say I'm successful; we're not hitting our numbers."

To dive into this topic of success, we're going to have to analyze what it means to be successful. Most people see success as a job or position that normally comes with monetary gain. When you're the CEO of a company, it's safe to say 99.9% of your employees would consider you to be successful. Here was an example where he was denying this success because of someone else he answered to.

Above the CEO was our parent company and shareholders. Let's call my CEO Dave. Dave had reached a pinnacle that so many dream of, the CEO of an international brand. However, Dave wasn't in a position to appreciate his success the way his employees saw it. Instead, his success was determined by an even higher group of decision-makers the employees hadn't even considered.

This made me question what I had to look forward to. The marketing job I was seeking was only my next step - my 6 month goal. Ten years down the road, I saw myself being CEO of the company. I envisioned myself standing in front of hundreds of people inspiring the tribe and leading the company to achieve new heights. Dave's answer about success made me question if that was what I really wanted.

The Successful

Would I end up doubting my own success too, once I had achieved it? This reminded me of a hidden level in a video game. You might work hard to get the highest position, only to see that there are even higher levels still to be conquered.

I understood Dave's response, but it probably wouldn't be the typical answer a CEO would give to a company employee. To me, Dave was an All-Star. He was a loyal family man and strong leader in our company. How was that not successful? Success is the places you go and impact you have on others along the way. To boil success down to hitting a quota seems disappointing. It's completely detached from the emotion of reaching that success pinnacle in the first place.

I didn't like the thought that I would always have to be looking up, making sure I was making other people happy. Success reduced to numbers wasn't how I wanted to view my achievements. Even when I failed at something, I still planned to consider myself a success.

Success is giving yourself the chance to fail. It's the person who puts themselves on stage hoping for a standing applause but ready to take crickets. Success is having morals and acting on them when no one is looking. Success comes from the heart. It's knowing you're walking down your purposeful path.

Success isn't a dream as much as it is a practice. You practice success by how you show up each day in the world. You practice it by persisting in the direction of your dreams. You practice it by making time for the people who are most important to you. You practice it by bringing others up alongside with you.

Success is having enough love for yourself to leave toxic relationships or situations, or to take space when you need to grow. Success is making a lot of money and understanding it's not about the dollars you earned. While abundance will come as you push forward, success to me is the person you become while you are striving for that ideal of success.

If you don't already consider yourself a success during the process, you won't once you "arrive" either. If you don't keep that appreciation for yourself, once you achieve the success you'll be anxiously looking for the next thing. You shouldn't ever be satisfied in life, but you should always feel successful. That's the mindset that allows you to be happy while expanding towards endless growth.

If Dave continued to not hit his numbers and he was let go, I would still consider him a success. I have no doubt that other people and companies would too.

I encourage you to write down what success means to you. Read it over and examine it. Does the definition make you feel empowered, or do you feel like it's a long way off? What would serve you better?

Make your definition of success something you can achieve this week, not in 10 years. Let's say that your definition of success is measured by how high up you make it in your company. That ultimate "success" will take awhile, but it has to start somewhere. What can you do this week as a stepping stone? Can you work harder on a project or introduce a new idea? If you did something this week that was in line with your goal, then it was a successful week.

Have a long term goal, but give yourself the chance to be successful right now. You'll see that mini successes start adding up, and soon enough you'll be the big success you always dreamed about. It starts with being successful NOW. How can you be a success today?

SECTION 3

SELF-DISCOVERY

CHAPTER 28

The Path

"What lies behind us and what lies before us are tiny matters compared to what lies within us." - Ralph Waldo Emerson

I mentioned the steps I took on my path while I strived to become a better version of myself in every aspect of my life - career and beyond. About the same time I broke up with Kelly and set up the Lunch with Lou experiment, I also signed up to compete in a triathlon. My days were spent working and training, and every night I lay in bed with smile on my face, feeling like I was crushing life. The tools and practices I learned were invaluable, but there was one practice specifically that set itself apart from the rest.

I mentioned journaling was the second most transformative habit I started, and this chapter is about the first. I could have never expected the effect this habit would have had on my life, and I could not be more excited about the popularity it's been gaining. What I'm referring to is the practice of meditation.

For those of you who have pre-conceived notions of a monk in Asia, hang in there with me. While yes, meditation can be that, its benefits are universal regardless of religion, no matter who you are, what you do, or how many yoga classes you've taken. The act of sitting still and quieting your mind has rewards that pour over into every aspect of life.

My experience with meditation opened the floodgates for the true essence of life to work its way in. Without meditation I wouldn't have written this book, and I wouldn't be anywhere near the person I am today. What meditation has allowed me to do is find a deeper meaning to my life. While you may not be looking for this, I know meditation would be helpful for you.

To understand my meditation journey, I should first explain why and how I got into it and what my spiritual beliefs were prior. I was raised Catholic and I went to church every Sunday with my family until I received confirmation, at which point I was given the choice of whether or not to go. I always believed in God or some sort of higher intelligence, but never understood why I had to go somewhere to show it, especially a church meeting where the priest or pastor didn't seem to be emotionally connected to what he or she was saying.

While I was away at college I got even further from being a church-going person, finding my higher purpose in a self-sabotaging lifestyle. When I started implementing changes in my life, I was far from feeling any kind of connection to a higher source, or even really caring if one existed.

I didn't start meditating to achieve enlightenment, open my chakras, or even just reduce stress. Like my other new habits, I started meditating just because *I saw successful people doing it.* In the books I read and conversations I had with entrepreneurs, it was becoming more evident that meditation was one of those hidden secrets to reach higher levels of achievement. Successful people from every walk of life meditate, which shows it can be for anyone. Billionaire investment bankers like Ray Dalio, Hollywood celebrities like Jennifer Aniston, and legendary musicians like Paul McCartney all meditate regularly. I was getting great results from trying other new things so I decided to give it a shot.

My first attempt was when I was still living with Kelly near the beach. One night when I was sure no one would be around, I put on some headphones and nestled into a cross legged seat on my floor with my back leaning against the wall. I set my timer for 5 minutes, closed my eyes, and off I went into meditation-land.

I wish I could tell you that 5 minutes turned into 5 hours, where I fell into a deep meditative state in which the meaning of life showed itself to me and my mind went to a different dimension. Well, it wasn't quite like that. I got through about 15 seconds until a voice popped in my head asking, "Am I doing this right?"

Like most people do when they begin meditating, I got frustrated with the random thoughts that kept coming into my mind, and questioned what the point was. How does sitting still and closing my eyes help me advance in my company? Where were the immediate benefits? I almost ended it all before I even got started.

Thankfully, I was able to change how I viewed the concept of meditation. Most beginners get frustrated with meditation because they think they should feel a certain way, or have a certain experience. They complain that they might not be doing it "right" which is completely false.

I realized that like any worthwhile practice, it takes time to see progress. If you've never played guitar and someone handed you one and said, "play some Jimi Hendrix", you'd laugh and tell them you need a lot more practice before you can do that. Well, the same is true for meditation. If you want to play the delicate notes of deep meditation, you first must start with one note, one breath, and one session at a time.

There's no wrong way to meditate, and you can't really fail at meditating; you just do it. By setting aside the time for your practice, you are meditating. You can measure your progress solely by your level of commitment. The more you commit, the more fruits of your labor you'll receive.

Although my first meditation ended after just two minutes, I kept at it. I figured that successful entrepreneurs like Ariana Huffington, Oprah Winfrey, and Russell Simmons had to be onto something. The whispers of success came through meditation, making their way into my life. This was the reason I kept meditating. I wanted the effects of it to spill over into my career. I saw myself as the poised leader who stayed calm under stress and was in the best position to solve problems. As I continued practicing, I was able to meditate for longer periods of time. It was slow at first, but I finally began to see the benefits.

Because I didn't meditate as a spiritual practice or consider myself a spiritual person, I had no way of preparing for the experiences I had. Before I move onto the topic of how meditation transformed my life and led to my huge leap of faith, I'd like to share a few meditation tips you can use right away. Whether you're a beginner, advanced meditator or anywhere in between, you're sure to find some value for your practice.

I haven't completed advanced training in a monastery for a certain type of meditation, but I've had a lot of personal experience and I can share practical advice about what I've learned.

The Path

What's so beautiful about meditation is that it's a life-long journey that only gets better as time goes on.

CHAPTER 29

The Technique

When I first started meditating, what worked well for me was listening to guided meditations with a person's voice leading me through the process. The main goal of meditation is to get out of your own head, so in the beginning it's helpful to hear words that help direct your mind onto a one-track focus. There are dozens of guided meditations available online you can try. I've created some guided meditations to help you; just search for 'Lou Redmond' on YouTube to find my channel.

If you'd like to experience other guided meditations, apps like Headspace, Insight Timer, Breathe, and Omvana all have meditations available for free and for purchase. I encourage you to check them out and see what works best for you.

Before you begin meditating you need to know the right way to sit, which is basically whatever makes you most comfortable. For a beginning meditator that's the first objective: get comfortable. If you're not comfortable, it's going to distract you from the main point of the practice which is to focus on your thoughts (or lack thereof). For me, 95% of my meditations are on a simple kitchen chair.

For this simple meditation posture, sit up straight with your feet flat on the ground. You can rest your hands on your knees, palms facing down. This provides a light push that helps keep your chest forward, and spine fully erect. You can also face your palms up in a more "receiving" gesture. I have a video on my YouTube channel which shows this basic position.

Meditation is sometimes described as conscious breathing. Effective breathing oxygenates the body and gets rid of toxic gases. This has a huge effect on your state of mind. It can make you excited or calm, stressed or happy. It can make your thinking clear or foggy. It is literally a power that can "forcedly direct your life."

Taking slow breaths in and out fills up your torso and allows the oxygen to provide a current of energy through your body. We normally go through our day completely unaware of our breath. It's what keeps us alive, but do we ever pay attention to it? Certain situations can trigger different breathing patterns without us even realizing it.

When we're nervous or anxious our breaths tend to become shorter and focused higher up in the chest. An "ideal" breath fills up the entire torso area, not just your upper chest. This kind of breathing can help ground and calm you during high-pressure situations. Becoming aware of how you're breathing is the quickest way to change the state of your body, which then changes the state of your mind. How crazy is it that the simplest God-given gift is what has the biggest impact on our physiological states?

Okay, back to your meditation practice. Are you sitting up straight in a chair yet? Take time to slowly inhale and exhale. With each inhalation, your belly should feel like it's filling up and rounding outward. The breath should slowly come in

The Technique

through the nose and then out and down throughout the body. On your exhale, it should feel like your lower back is gently pushing down against the chair. This breathing pattern creates a natural straightening of the spine.

Your breathing should be kept constant - in through the nose and then out and down through the body. With your eyes closed, focus your gaze on the area in between your eyebrows. Some cultures teach that this area is the location of your third eye and that by focusing here, you are helping to increase your intuitive sense. Close your eyes right now and practice focusing your gaze on this area. If you strain or feel like you're squinting, you're trying too hard. You should have a soft relaxed gaze, not an intense one.

Now that you have your gaze focused and your feet flat, make sure you keep your chin level to the ground. Your back should be away from the back of the chair but if that begins to strain you too much, it's better to let yourself be comfortable than to forego the meditation altogether. Do what works for you.

Now that you're in position, it's time to focus on your breath. Start your meditation with a few deep inhales and exhales, enough to fully settle into the posture. With each inhale feel your body expand outwards. With each exhale, imagine the tension leaving your body. Work your way from the top of your head all the way down your body, releasing tension in each area as you go. For example on the inhale, think about your neck and shoulders rising up, and then on the exhale, relax your neck and shoulders as you think about tension leaving this area of your body.

Putting your full attention on each inhale and exhale is the most common practice for beginners, but it may end up becoming boring to you. In my meditation classes, I teach a method that creates an awareness of the surroundings. I find this is another great way for beginners to start.

If you're indoors, you could try this by first listening specifically for any cars driving by, people or machinery outside. Focus on this for about two minutes. Then, stop focusing on these sounds and begin to listen to the sounds inside. Is the heat or air conditioning on? Can you hear a clock ticking, the fridge humming, or any other sounds? Even if you don't hear anything, you're training your mind to focus your attention.

After you've done this for about two minutes, now listen for sounds of nature. Are there birds chirping outside? Is it a stormy day? Can you hear the wind blowing up against the shutters? This focus should last another few minutes until finally you bring it all together.

Bring in your focus of the outside traffic and other sounds, sounds inside your home, nature sounds, everything that you heard. Listen to it all at once, like an orchestra that's playing around you. Hear each chord ring out, and understand that you are tuning into the orchestra of life. This life is happening all around you at the same time. Realize that you are not separate from it. You are a part of it, inside it.

As you're focusing your attention on the melody of life, feel yourself in the middle playing an integral part. Relish in the glory that you are part of the magic that is moving through this earth and beyond. Picture yourself in meditation as the center of the Universe, connected to everything that makes it up.

This practice can work even better when you meditate outside, where you can bring in the sounds of nature even more. You can feel the wind on your skin and see the light of the sun through your eyelids. These are just more instruments for your repertoire.

The Technique

Another suggestion would be to put on a favorite song or listen to classical music. While meditating, notice each instrument individually, and focus on them one at a time. After you've done this, bring them all together as one orchestra, one sound.

I would also suggest searching binaural beats on YouTube to listen to. Binaural beats are sound waves specifically tailored to stimulate brain function, and help you get into a deeper meditation faster.

If this type of meditation technique doesn't seem to work for you the first time, don't worry. It takes practice just like any other skill. Also, you may find another technique that resonates with you more. I suggest you keep yourself open to all kinds of techniques, and see what works best for you.

Here's a review of the basics for a sitting meditation:

1. Feet Flat & Spine Straight
2. Hands on Knees
3. Breathe in through the nose, fill up the entire torso
4. Breathe out through the nose and down through the body
5. Repeat

As for the amount of time you should dedicate to meditation, I suggest that you set easy goals. Start with 1 minute a day and then increase the time from there. The key is consistency and setting the time aside to do it every day. You're never too busy to find a few minutes in your day to meditate.

An old Zen quote goes something like this: "You should sit in meditation for 20 minutes a day. If you think you're too busy, you should sit for 2 hours."

Meditation helps you quiet your focus on your outer world and go within. When you do this you'll find a deeper meaning and connection to life. It's in the silence that you can hear more clearly the whispers guiding you to your deepest levels of fulfillment. Your true nature - Your Truth - can be accessed directly through this practice. You'll read in the upcoming chapters how it opened me to mine.

Meditation is my #1 recommendation to people no matter what they're looking to achieve. Whether it's to decrease stress, find a sense of purpose, get better sleep, or even lose weight: meditation is an easy, natural path to an overall sense of well-being and personal insight.

CHAPTER 30

The Backstory

"If you'd be a real seeker of truth, it is necessary that at least once in your life you doubt, as far as possible, all things." - Rene Descartes

I've never had formal meditation training, but I consider myself to be an expert level meditator. I've advanced in my practice and I've had experiences that many seasoned meditators would be happy to achieve. It was through these experiences that I developed a deep love for - and connection with - meditation.

The story I'm about to tell explains some of these experiences. It's a touching story for me, and may not be believable to you. This is something I've come to accept: it's my personal experience and the best I can do is to tell it from my perspective and encourage others to meditate too. While it might be difficult to describe fully, I find some reassurance in this quote:

"For those who have experienced, no words are necessary. For those who haven't, no words are possible."- Dr. Wayne Dyer

If you haven't had an experience similar to those I describe here, I understand they might be hard to understand on an "empathic" level. My main purpose for writing this book is to share the sequence of events that occurred in a short period of time and the effect they had on me. These experiences are what brought me a level of transformation which I didn't anticipate and couldn't have prepared for.

As I mentioned earlier, I wasn't a spiritual person and I wasn't seeking spiritual wisdom. I hadn't even been meditating long enough for there to be an expected correlation between my practice and my experiences. I actually laughed at people who had "found God", Jesus or whatever, changing their lives and considering themselves, "Born Again." So before you think I might be someone in that category, I'll say up front...it did seem a little like taking on a new life, but not in the same way.

I should note here that I use the term God and Universe interchangeably. There's no right word for me, just an awareness of a higher intelligence that surrounds us all. I did "find" God, but it wasn't like He/She/It was just hiding in the backyard. The reality isn't something you see, it's something you experience. Just like your body digests food without you having to think about it, it's possible to just *know* when insights, feelings and awareness occur.

I began meditating in July 2014. I started slowly. I didn't get excited about it like I did with my other new habits of reading and journaling. I considered myself "not good" at meditating, and only tried it a handful of times over the first few months.

I gained some momentum when I moved out into my own space, but even then it wasn't much. I went from meditating twice a month to maybe once a week, then twice a week. While I recommend that you should meditate for at least a few

The Backstory

minutes each day, I didn't have that practice when I first started meditating.

This is why my experiences with meditation baffle me so much. I wasn't even focused on meditation as a spiritual practice; I just thought it would help be more successful at work. I actually enjoyed the *idea* of meditating more than actually sitting down and doing it. It wasn't until six months later that I learned what meditation was all about. My "Aha" moment came, and when it hit, it came with the force of a hurricane.

I was particularly amazed because as I mentioned earlier, I wasn't the type to believe in religion or spirituality. In fact, just two weeks before my "Aha" moment, I watched the documentary "Zeitgeist" and decided that I was in complete agreement with the film. The documentary brought up the idea that all religions are based on myth, made up in the same way corporations are formed today. It argued that religion was a business, backing it up with logical statements about why God doesn't exist. It all made sense to me; I agreed that God didn't exist and all this stuff about God had just been made up.

This was just a few days before the Christmas holiday. As I sat during Christmas Eve mass in the Church I grew up attending, I completely denied all of it. I sat there thinking it was really all just made up. I remember choosing not to receive communion because I had a strong stance that we were all just being fooled. And so it was on Christmas Eve that I decided there was no God. That probably helps explain how much I *wasn't* looking for the experiences that followed.

That's when things got interesting...

CHAPTER 31

The Question

"It is impossible for a man to learn what he thinks he already knows." – Epictetus

It was mid-morning in Palm Springs California where I was journaling at a small, hip coffee shop. I was in town visiting some friends for the New Year's holiday. The day before had been spent nursing my New Year's Eve hangover, but after that time to recoup and a sober night with a good night's sleep, I was feeling fantastic.

My plan was to head back to San Diego to enjoy what was left of the New Year's weekend, but I suddenly got an idea to go on a hike alone; something I'd never done before. The desert had always given me a sense of peace and serenity, and I thought it would be a perfect time to enjoy nature, outside in the environment I loved.

Find Your Truth

I knew that Joshua Tree National Park was nearby and I had an image of myself meditating high on top of a mountain, overlooking a sea of ridged landscape. I was giddy at the thought of making this image come to fruition. I decided to follow through on the idea and venture out on this new experience. I searched on my phone for a trail that looked enticing, and off I went.

After parking at the trailhead lot I started out on my solo climb. With backpack strapped, I felt like a warrior heading into the adventures of battle. I knew going into it that I wanted to go off the trail and create my own path to the top. I walked along a river route for the first hundred yards until my summit came into view. It looked challenging, but doable. I wasted no time and headed off toward the base.

I paused at the base to tighten up my backpack and re-lace my shoes. I set sight on my target and eagerly began my ascent. The terrain started out modestly. I looked straight ahead, starting out strong. As the slope started to increase, it demanded a greater level of concentration. No longer could I look up at my destination, but I had to stay focused on what was directly in front of me. One false step could leave me in danger with no one to come to my rescue.

A slap of realization came to me as I realized a metaphor about life: if you focus too much on your destination, looking too far into the future, you could trip and fall because of what's right in front of you. It's when you focus on what's directly at hand that you become fully "present". That's when you're able to use all of your faculties, both mental and physical. This method makes it clearer to navigate; one rock and one task at a time; it's the very definition of "mindfulness". This was just the beginning of what became a very insightful climb.

I continued up the mountain, my breaths getting shorter with each inclining step. Needing a break, I picked out a spot

The Question

to begin my first meditation. It was a shaded area beneath a desolate tree that was growing sideways out of the ground. I sat on a rock that allowed me to put my feet flat on the ground. I slowed down my breath and moved into my meditation "flow".

Within the first few breaths I could tell this meditation was different than any I had experienced before. My mind wasn't shouting at me, telling me I suck or that I was doing it wrong. My usual brain chatter was silenced, and I was in a state of calm and peace. There were no fretting thoughts about past events or worries about projects at work I needed to finish. I felt completely in the moment.

I somehow went into a trance-like state, tuning into my breath which electrified my whole body. It was then that a thought entered my consciousness, just two words out of nowhere –"You're Fulfilled". Without trying to analyze or interpret the meaning, I just started repeating them over and over. "You're fulfilled." ..."You're fulfilled." The calmness I felt intensified and I slowly became more aware again of my surroundings.

As I opened my eyes, I noticed that everything around me looked different. There seemed to be a radiance in the air that I hadn't noticed before. My meditation was 20 minutes, which was the longest I had ever meditated alone without guidance. Overjoyed by the length of my meditation and the insightful words, I continued on my hike and scoped out my next resting spot.

In the distance, a solid rock jutted out of the side of the mountain slope like it could be a lookout peak for wolves. It seemed to be the ideal place I had pictured for my mediation. I trekked briskly, excited to begin another meditation after the fascinating experience from the previous one.

Find Your Truth

I got to the rock, but this time there was no way for me to have my feet flat on the ground. I had to sit cross-legged, something I'd never been comfortable doing. I moved into position, surprised at the ease in which I was able to re-enter the same trance-like state.

Once the calmness set in, I started repeating the phrase "You're Fulfilled" again. It was then that the rest of the words came clearly to my mind which completed the sentence. The words were clear and simple: "You're fulfilled *at your core*" and then again, repeated: "You're fulfilled at your core."

At that moment, a wave of understanding washed over me. I realized the phrase "You're fulfilled at your core" meant that I didn't need anything outside myself to truly be fulfilled. I had all I needed, deep within the core of my being. I understood that no job or accomplishment would bring me the fulfillment that was already inside me. I just hadn't realized it until that moment.

I smiled in awe and appreciation for these powerful messages. My second meditation lasted about as long as the previous one. I was in a beautiful spot looking towards the south end of the mountain range. My view to my destination at the north end was blocked, so I knew I had to continue upward. I looked up and picked out one last peak to climb at the top of the hill.

This time the path looked sketchy and more difficult to navigate. I was feeling in my "zone" so I didn't waste time thinking about it. I was captivated by each moment. Every step I took felt natural, as if I were being guided, in the flow. I moved quickly to the top in this manner.

I reached the peak I had seen at the beginning of my hike; my heart was beating quickly. I paused to take in all the terrain I had scaled, doing a 180-degree scan of my surroundings. I was deeply moved by the beauty of it all, the sea of ridged landscape. I couldn't believe I had reached the exact spot I had set

The Question

out to find, and I felt elated because of my personal insights during meditation.

Instead of doing another meditation, I took out my journal to write down the things I had just experienced. I wrote about what I had understood "You're fulfilled at your core" to mean. Intuitively, I somehow knew this meant that God was inside each of us, and that deep down, that's what really makes us fulfilled.

As I continued writing, I started feeling a strong emotional connection with the concept of being a father. In the weeks prior, I had been brought to tears on multiple occasions when watching fathers and sons happily playing together in the park or families relaxing and talking with their children. These encounters made me think about how I wanted to raise my kids, and what kind of father I would be one day.

Just the day before in fact, I had been sitting hung-over at a coffee shop, watching a family enjoy each other's company and celebrating their New Year together. Here's my journal entry from that day:

1/1/15

"I'm sitting outside having coffee in Palm Springs right now. Palm trees and mountains in the background. This place is just so relaxing. I love it...I'm watching a family enjoy their morning together. Seems like young couples with a couple of kids and their grandparents. When I'm a Dad I never want to be so hungover I can't give full attention to my kids. I started missing Kelly again this morning. When I feel like shit and am lonely: that always happens. We are such good friends. She is literally the perfect girl in so many ways."

Then on the mountain peak I wrote the following journal entry that led to an amazing experience of feeling "spirit" for myself:

1/2/15

"I'm sitting at the top of my own mountain right now, looking into a sea of endless peaks and dips. It's absolutely gorgeous. I'm panting a little because it took some focus getting up here. It taught me a lesson. You need to focus entirely on what's directly in front of you. If I was looking up at the rock, I would/could lose my footing and have bad consequences. I needed to be completely present in the moment. LOOKING AHEAD IS DETRIMENTAL. I did some meditating on my way up. At my first stop it came to me to start chanting, "You're Fulfilled." At my next stop I chanted or dictated I should say, "You're Fulfilled at your Core." Meaning God is inside us, at our backbone we were put on this earth for a real reason. I'm so lucky to see this so clearly. I'd like to make another pledge to my sons or daughters...."

As I wrote the last line of that journal entry, it was if the sky opened up and it suddenly dawned on me what my pledge meant; what it needed to be. I stopped my writing, laid my journal down on my lap, and looked up curiously at the sky. I sat there in a state of confusion, trying to figure out the feeling that was coming over me. I realized I was scared. Tears began welling up in my eyes.

The past several months had been a huge life transformation for me, and I felt like I was crushing it from every angle. I recently got the promotion I had been pursuing and I felt like I was getting closer to finding my true purpose and making my personal impact.

Although life was going great, it seemed like I was being tested on the mountain. It was like the sky I was looking up at

The Question

was looking back down saying, "Lou you've been doing great, you really have, but do you really want it? Do you want all that life has in store for you?"

If you had been asked this question, how would you answer? I'll ask it here: do you want everything life has in store for you? Are you willing to pay the price to get it?

The word that came clearly to me at that moment was "transcend." It was as if the Universe was asking me: "Do you want to transcend to the next level of life?" Of course I wanted to transcend, but I also realized what that transcendence was going to cost me.

I felt strongly that I was being challenged to break the habit I had clung to for ten years; the same habit that had plagued my family name and had caused a lot of problems and pain for me and my loved ones. I felt like it was time for me to write these powerful words to my future children: "On this day, January 2nd 2015th...on this day, I, Louis Redmond - STOP DRINKING."

CHAPTER 32

The Answer

"Not until we are lost do we begin to understand ourselves."
– Henry David Thoreau

Really? Could I stop drinking? Could I commit to what I thought was an insurmountable challenge? Was this really the price I had to pay to get all that life had in store for me? There was only one way to know for sure: I had to answer the question and take that step.

I knew I was determined enough to take it on. All I had to do next was to write it down and make the commitment to myself in my journal. That sounded easy, but I honestly didn't know if I could do it. I didn't know if I could truly handle myself in a world without drinking AT ALL. I stood there looking out on the horizon, searching in the depth of my being for the push to say yes.

As I returned back to the idea of my future children, I thought of what little of a man I would be if I refused to accept the challenge. The time was right, and I felt like it was now or never. I was being called upon to make the biggest decision of my life, and those types of callings come with the greatest amount of fear. They also come with the most uncertainty about the future.

Once I asked myself the question of whether or not I could rise to the challenge, I already knew the answer. I don't usually back down from a challenge and this particular one came from a higher source; a deeper place within me. It seemed that God, the Universe, Angels, Love...whatever you want to call it...it was offering me some kind of challenge. The test was being held, and it was pass or fail.

I let go of my trepidation, battled through my fear, and looked inside myself, then looked back down at my journal and finished writing the sentence: "To my future sons or daughters, on this day, I STOP DRINKING."

As I added a final period to the sentence and smacked my journal shut, a release and exuberance came over me that was impossible to put into words. It was the most beautiful experience of my life up to that point. This ecstatic feeling washed over me, and I began sobbing. For lack of better words, it felt like my entire soul opened up. I felt some type of ethereal sense of lightness that I hadn't known was possible.

I had answered the question and accepted the challenge, and was being rewarded with this incredible feeling that not even ecstasy could match by comparison. With tears streaming down my face, I reached both arms up and out wide, yelling out to the sky the words "THANK YOU!!!"

It was a moment I will never forget. It was a revelation that not only was it time for me to stop drinking, but that there was a higher force out there. I felt so unendingly blessed to have found it, to have *experienced* it.

The experience was unlike anything I could have imagined. I took a few more minutes to take in the mountain range and

The Answer

focus on the joy and gratitude I was feeling about what was happening. Just as I was ready to leave, a bee flew to me, hovering around my left knee. Considering I was on top of a desert mountain, it didn't seem like a place for bees so I made a mental note of it. With gratitude coming as if from my bones, appreciation pouring from my soul, it was time to head back down to real life.

I climbed down the mountain with the lightness of a feather. In complete control of my footing, I moved quickly and with grace. When I reached the bottom, I ran back to the trailhead with my arms outstretched like an airplane and a smile that stretched ear to ear.

I got in my car and started to drive back to San Diego. It was then that the extremity of what I had committed to actually hit me. Could I really just stop drinking, just like that? Does it have to be forever? Forever seemed like a long time. Still grateful for the experience, I decided to just take on this challenge day by day.

During the drive all I could think about was how deeply spiritual my experience had been, almost to the point that I could hardly believe it. Without even looking for an experience like that I was shown a deep look into *my truth*. I was excited to see where this new life would lead me. Little did I know what more the next few days had in store.

CHAPTER 33

The Infinite Realization

"And those who were seen dancing were thought to be insane by those who could not hear the music." - Friedrich Nietzsche

The Sunday morning after my experience at Joshua Tree, I was still in awe. I hadn't told anyone the full story yet and how it had affected me, but I was aching to get it off my chest. When something as profound as that happens, you just need to tell someone. What I learned further down the road was that you have to be careful who you talk to.

Some people aren't ready to hear about epiphanies, synchronicities, or finding God on a mountain. Something like that just isn't considered normal to most people. If you've had a similar experience and tried talking to people about it, you understand. Trying to explain such a uniquely personal or spiritual experience to another person who hasn't had the same experience is close to impossible. However, when you're going through it, talking about it is exactly what you need the most.

I didn't have anyone to share this experience with at the time. That's one reason why I felt called to share this story with other people. I listen to others' stories of profound experiences and revelations because I know how hard it can be going at it alone. It's a completely new world you find yourself in. With something so unfamiliar and that happens so fast, it's natural to feel lost.

Luckily I told the story to two friends who wouldn't look at me like I had three heads. That conversation is what gave me the inspiration to travel on to the next leg of my spiritual journey. On that day I decided to take a drive up the I-5 freeway to a very special place I had heard about that morning- the Paramahansa Yogananda's Self Realization Fellowship gardens in Encinitas, CA.

The gardens are open to the public and the grounds offer a peaceful place to walk, enjoy the beauty of nature, and meditate. It was just two days after my meditations on the mountain, and because I wanted to continue to embrace and learn from this new world that had opened up to me, it seemed like the perfect place to spend my Sunday afternoon.

I was sitting on a bench at the SRF grounds and when I closed my eyes to get into my place of deep calm and serenity, I found that I was able to instantly. After 20 minutes of a simple breathing meditation, I opened my eyes and had the experience again of being greeted with vibrant surroundings. It seemed that my senses were more acute, that I had a higher level of awareness for the beauty around me. Even the colors of the flowers seemed brighter and more potent. I stood up slowly and walked through this majestic beauty of Mother Nature.

The Infinite Realization

With each step I took, I felt rooted deeper into the ground. The flowers seemed to radiate a beauty that nearly swept me away. I walked slowly, smelling the air and taking in all that was around me. I was in a state of pure appreciation for nature's beauty. Not just appreciation, but I felt a connection to my surroundings in a way I'd never experienced before. No longer did I feel separate from the trees and plants, but I felt as if we were one. I was a part of it, a part of nature. I *was* nature.

I was created from nature just like any other plant or animal so on some level, this feeling of oneness made perfect sense; we came from the same source. I walked around the bend then looked over the ocean. The sun electrified the cool water with its sparkling rays. I sat down on a bench and began another meditation.

I went into a 30 minute trance-like state that felt like one minute. As I came out of the meditation, my attention was drawn to the coastal cliffs that jutted out both to the north and south. I stood up to get a better view and as I looked around in wonder at the vast and beautiful landscape, I couldn't help but think of my place in it all. The world was so big, with so many people and so many places to see. My musings naturally begged the question: "What have I done with my time here?"

A little sadness came over me when I considered how I'd been spending my time. Each of us has a finite number of days of life on this planet, and I wondered how I was using those days if I were just cooped up in an office. A feeling of love then wafted over me, as I wondered who I was helping during my time here. I clearly saw how insignificant my existence was in the larger order of things. It was that same insignificance that ignited a glorious sense of freedom.

How could I NOT choose to live life to the fullest? How could I not take full advantage of the precious days while I had them? I sat back down on the bench in a state of wonder and bliss. An instant later, there it was again; a bee circling around my left knee just as the bee had done at the top of the mountain. While I still wasn't sure of its significance, I had a strong sense that it shouldn't be dismissed as coincidence. I felt a deeper instinct that there was some kind of message in it yet to be understood, and I was reminded of my connection with nature.

My life was shifting in front of my eyes and I sat back, feeling the most powerful love I'd ever felt. It was a love that emanated out of every part of my being. I felt one with it all, and somehow connected to another higher plane of existence. If someone had put me on a scale at that time I would have said I weighed 5 ounces. I felt so light that it wouldn't have surprised me if I had been carried away by the wind, along the Pacific coast.

There was only one thing I felt, one word on my mind. It was what all the mystics and cliché memes refer to; what many people want but don't understand. It's where we came from and where we're going. It was the best feeling, best expression available in the entire Universe. It's why we were created and what we are. It was *Love*.

CHAPTER 34

The Synchronicities

I left the meditation gardens and made my way on a drive down the San Diego Freeway. I felt abundance radiating from within me. I fully appreciated the opportunity to celebrate this spectacular day. I veered off the road to grab lunch at a fancy restaurant along the beach. Being a bit pricey, it was the type of restaurant I would typically save for a special date. Spontaneously going alone was way out of character, but I felt great: I just wanted to celebrate this feeling, and share it with others.

As I bit down into my seared tuna with tarragon crème sauce, the flavors electrified my body. I sat alone, gazing out at the patrons in the restaurant. I felt a heightened sense that some of them were taking notice of me in a way that seemed curious, inquisitive. I imagined they could be thinking: "Who is this guy? There seems to be something mysterious about him."

The people who came near me smiled and seemed to light up. I felt like some kind of celebrity with the attention that seemed to be directed my way. It was as if they could sense something special had happened, but weren't able to define it. It was as new to them as it was to me.

I finished up my lunch and continued my journey south towards San Diego, making another stop for afternoon tea at a coffee shop in La Jolla. I sat at the corner table and peered out the window; my view consisted of coastal homes and a tethered glimpse of blue ocean. Sipping my lavender chamomile tea I was brought back to a time just six months earlier. I had been sitting at that same place with Kelly, reading *Outwitting the Devil*, the book that literally changed my life.

I was there alone on this occasion, feeling as high as ever but I couldn't help but miss Kelly. My "highest self" recognized her as one of the purest souls I'd ever been in contact with, and in my reverie, I felt like she could be the perfect companion.

I stopped reminiscing about Kelly and got present to my surroundings. A man and woman were on a first date at the table next to me. I could tell it was a first date by the awkwardness of their conversation. The man started explaining how he'd had to quit drinking for two weeks, lamenting how horrible it had been. A light bulb went off in my head as I thought about how ridiculous that actually seemed to me. This man couldn't enjoy two weeks without drinking? I took it as a sign that I'd made a wise choice to jump into a new life without alcohol.

Overhearing their conversation hit home because I knew in past days, that man could have easily been me. I was the one waiting for the next weekend bender, the next party, the next time I could drink my face off and "enjoy" life. Although I knew it came with a price, that never stopped me. It was through meeting new people and seeing life from a different perspective that I saw how degenerating and miserable that type of existence was. Sure, it could be fun every so often, but

The Synchronicities

to live life for the weekends and nothing else seemed like a slow, spiritual suicide.

This was another example in my life of how everything seemed to be falling into place. It all made sense. I started journaling in the coffee shop and four words kept coming to mind: "*I figured it out.*" The thought came to me that this life had all been a game and somehow I stumbled on the secret code. I felt like my new perspectives from the past few months were coming to a culmination. I felt like something big was about to happen.

My head was so much clearer without alcohol. Here's my journal entry at the coffee shop: "*As long as I don't drink my mind is an above average thinking being, capable of the highest potential....I'm two steps closer to my purpose. There is one last hurdle to find it. I can feel it so clearly.*" I wasn't sure what the hurdle would be, but I knew I was close to something. The new experiences and connectedness to all things was leading me somewhere. I didn't ask questions, I just went with it, following my heart. I was fully consumed by the dream I was living.

The sun was setting when I continued my drive home. It was the kind of sunset you never forget; the sun lit the entire sky a majestic purple color. The grace of a higher power at work was almost tangible. I held so much gratitude in my heart that I couldn't help but cry. It was an epic ending to another intensely moving day. I didn't know exactly what was going on, but I knew that someday it would all make sense.

That night in bed I laid my head down, overcome with gratitude for the past three days. I couldn't wait to get up the next morning and share this amazing feeling with my co-workers. That was, until I got a text that changed the course of my life, once again.

CHAPTER 35

The Text

"This is your life. Do what you want and do it often.
If you don't like something, change it.
If you don't like your job, quit.
If you don't have enough time, stop watching TV.
If you are looking for the love of your life, stop; they will be waiting for you when you start doing things you love.
Stop over-analyzing, life is simple.
All emotions are beautiful.
When you eat, appreciate every last bite.
Life is simple.
Open your heart, mind and arms to new things and people; we are united in our differences.
Ask the next person you see what their passion is and share your inspiring dream with them.
Travel often; getting lost will help you find yourself.
Some opportunities only come once, seize them.
Life is about the people you meet and the things you create with them, so go out and start creating.

Life is short, live your dream and wear your passion." - The Holstee Manifesto

At 9:00 PM just as I was about to fall asleep, I was jolted back to life by the buzz of my phone. I grabbed it and saw a text from Kelly. The message was a picture of her journal. She had written out the Holstee Manifesto. I forced myself awake so I could understand what I was reading.

After reading through it, I was appreciative that she had sent me such beautiful words but I felt drained from such an intense day, so I put my head back down to get some sleep. I was finding it difficult because one line from the Manifesto kept coming into my mind: "If you don't like your job, quit."

I wondered why this resonated so strongly within me. I liked my job. I liked my company and I liked where my life was heading. There was something about that line that stuck with me though. I started thinking about what would happen if I actually did quit my job. This new promotion was taking up much more of my time than the previous one, and I was losing the time I previously had available for reading and personal growth. That was time I truly cherished, but wasn't my original reason for spending time on personal growth so that I could get the job in the first place?

The more I thought about it, the more things didn't add up. I knew the marketing position wasn't my end goal and it certainly wasn't my life's purpose. I wasn't completely sold that it was the job which would get me closer to my purpose either. The fact that I was working at least 50 hours a week served as a convenient excuse for letting loose and partying on the weekends, and I was starting to fall back into some old patterns. I had started nursing hangovers again with my new job, rather than enjoying crushing life.

The Text

That would all change now after what happened. With my newfound life without alcohol, I started feeling very out of place with my promotion. Our big trade show was two weeks away and I knew there would be plenty of drinking with co-workers and clients. This only added to my fear of my new job trajectory and where it would lead. But quit? I couldn't quit a new job two months in, leaving everyone scurrying to pick up the pieces. Or could I? Where was my sense of loyalty and commitment? I'd watched people be fired on the spot without much explanation, so was there really anything I owed the company?

I told myself the most reasonable thing would be to give them a two weeks' notice and go from there. I thought about that, but knew it would be impossible. I was sure they'd pull out all the stops to make it difficult and I'd likely get talked out of it by my manager, the CEO, and everyone else who was counting on me. My decision wouldn't make any sense to them, and there would be no way that I could make them understand where I was coming from.

Explaining that I had found God and that I felt there was a different master plan for me would get me admitted to a mental hospital. I felt I had a big responsibility to fulfill, even though I wasn't quite sure what it was, and I had the feeling like I couldn't waste another second. The more I thought about the idea, the more momentum it gained. I rehearsed how I would give my notice via email. I thought that if I wrote it well, somehow they would understand.

What was I going to do if I did quit? I still had to pay the bills, right? I had absolutely no money saved, so this should probably have concerned me more at the time. For some reason, I wasn't worried. During that day at the meditation gardens and while I contemplated the insignificance of life, I knew

I needed to be of service. I needed to do more, to make a contribution. I had no idea what that meant, or how I was going to do it. I had no idea what I was going to do to afford to live, but something undeniable was pushing me to find out. I wrestled most of the night with the thought of quitting my job. After waking up from just one hour of sleep, I knew I wasn't ready just yet. I was still feeling great from my recent experiences. I felt so much love inside that I was determined to go to work and try to spread the joy I was feeling to everyone there. I thought they would see the joy I was radiating and join in on the ride. After that, we'd be riding high and looking to make more of a positive impact with our lives and on the people around us. That's what I thought, but that's not exactly how things played out.

CHAPTER 36

The Disconnect

"It is no measure of health to be well adjusted to a profoundly sick society." - Jiddu Krishnamurti

I drove to work the next morning in silent anticipation. Everyone was getting back from their holiday vacations, and I felt sure they'd be bubbling with as much excitement to be back in the office as I was. I walked up the stairs and was greeted by the CEO's secretary. I gave her a big smile and bright eyed "Good Morning!" I received back a hasty hello; she seemed to be more focused on the work she needed to catch up with.

At my desk I started going through and replying to some emails. I replaced my usual "Good Morning" email salutation with "Great Morning!" I knew it was out of the ordinary, but I needed to express my positive mental state or I felt like I would just burst. The issue was that no one seemed to be on my same wavelength.

Find Your Truth

As the day progressed, I starting noticing a disconnect in my co-workers' faces that I hadn't noticed before. It seemed like they were frustrated in a way they weren't even aware of. They didn't seem to be present in real time. Their minds were elsewhere, concerned about meeting deadlines and making sure their tasks got done.

Their demeanor felt strangely different from mine. The more people I interacted with, the more my mood changed incrementally each time, to match theirs. As the morning progressed, I noticed more than just a disconnect with others; I felt a disconnect with my work too.

For example, I was sitting in a meeting discussing what graphics we were going to use for a display, and with the mood in the room, we might as well have been talking about chemotherapy treatment. We were taking everything so seriously, but for what? What good were we actually doing?

Back at my desk, I pondered that question. Was I going to be able to do some kind of good here? We made the same expensive toys each year and marketed our products like they were going to make someone's golf game even better than the last. While my heart had always been in the game, something seemed to be misaligned now. I questioned why people were starving in many places of the world, yet we were all breaking our backs helping rich white guys hit a white ball two yards further. Was this really the best use of my time?

My mind raced all day. I couldn't fight the feeling that I needed to get out at some point. All I could think about was how, and if quitting would be feasible. I wanted someone to talk to who understood what I was going through. That's when I felt compelled to reach out to Jorge.

I knew Jorge through one of my good friends. They had gone to college together so I occasionally partied with him but we were never directly connected. Over Facebook, I noticed

The Disconnect

Jorge had left the country and had started a group called World Travelers Association. The mission of World Travelers Association was "adventure travel for a cause." They hosted travel retreats that focused on both adventure and community service. Knowing that Jorge was a frat party kid like I was, I figured he might have had a similar awakening for him to choose such a different path.

I sent Jorge a message and shared some of the spiritual experiences I was going through with him, in hopes that I might have someone who could relate. I didn't get an immediate response back, so my workday continued uneasily as before. The tipping point came during a meeting at the end of the day.

I was sitting in a conference room where we were discussing a party we were throwing for one of our sponsors. The topic was about who we were going to invite to make a good impression. We wanted to make sure the right people were there to benefit the company's publicity. It was superficial at best.

As the meeting continued, my manger joked about having cocaine and molly at the party. When I heard this, I felt like I had just stepped into the Twilight Zone. Never before had the topic of these two drugs came up at work, let alone by a manager. I took this as another indication that I should leave, that I was no longer in a place that would support my new choices.

I got back to my desk after the meeting and thought long and hard again about quitting. My idea was still to quit from home, with an email message. It could have seemed like a cowardly way to quit, but in my heart I knew there was no other way. If I quit, I'd need to give a personal explanation to a few people who had played a big role in me getting the promotion in the first place.

It was 7:00 PM and most everyone on the second floor had gone home for the day. I wrote heartfelt letters to the CEO, my managers, and my mentor, trying to explain my decision. The caveat in each letter was that I knew there would be no way they could understand. I still was unsure if I was going to follow through, so I left the letters under my keyboard in case I decided at the last minute to change my mind.

I packed up the items I wanted to take with me and started to leave. I noticed that the light was still on in the CEO's office. The thought of quitting was eating away at me from inside, and I wanted so badly to tell someone what I was thinking about doing. I decided to step into his office to let him know what was going through my mind. I thought for sure I could explain myself and be understood.

As I walked by and poked my head into his office, he was nowhere to be found so I continued down the stairs to leave. I pushed through the double glass doors out into the dark night. The doors swung symmetrically as I made my departure into the night, and into my uncertain future. Looking back I realized that had the CEO been there, I might not be writing this.

In an attempt to find answers, I drove down to my old thinking spot on Mission Bay. I meditated, prayed, searched for some kind of certainty from within, but it wasn't there. What kept coming up was that I didn't know the next time this opportunity to leave would come up again; I had to do it now.

I had a vision of myself ten years in the future. The man was a version of me who hadn't taken the leap and was still in the same spot. He was going through another experience and again had the chance to jump. Did I want to be the guy who waited ten years? It was clear that I had to do this, or I'd essentially be putting my life on hold.

I got back to my apartment at 9:00 PM, completely exhausted. My mind was too frazzled to be able to make a firm

The Disconnect

decision, which made me anxious. I thought about relieving some of my anxiety by reaching out to Kelly and explaining what was going through my mind about quitting my job.

I grabbed the phone and began typing a text message to Kelly, but something stopped me. I turned my phone off and told myself, "No. If I'm going to do this, it has to be fully on me. I can't try to bring anyone else into this."

It was then I decided to set my alarm for 5:00 AM, and see how I felt in the morning. I was confused and scared, but fortunately exhaustion won out, and I fell into a deep sleep.

Next up - The craziest day of my life.

CHAPTER 37

The Departure

"When you walk to the edge of all the light you have and take that first step into the darkness of the unknown, you must believe that one of two things will happen. There will be something solid for you to stand upon or you will be taught to fly."– Patrick Overton

I woke up suddenly in the middle of the night and turned over to look at my phone. It was 3:00 AM on the dot, and I noticed that Jorge had responded back. I jumped out of bed and quickly swiped my phone to read the message.

Jorge's response was one of understanding. He explained he had a similar experience in college that gave him the vision of starting a volunteer organization and traveling the world for a greater cause. During this time of upheaval and transition in my life, that response meant everything to me and immediately got me out of bed, two hours before my alarm was set to go off.

As I made coffee and got my morning started, I felt a deeper sense of clarity than I had the night before. Quitting my job was more real than ever; I just had to get over one last hurdle. I knew before taking the leap that I wanted to tell my parents what I was about to do. I had some trepidation they might try to discourage me, but it didn't stop me from calling.

As you might guess, it took them by surprise. I was grilled with the typical questions, the most obvious being "What are you going to do for money?" I didn't have an answer, but I told them how much it felt like something I really had to do. I explained my desire to help others, and to travel. I told them I knew it would be hard for them to understand, and asked for their support.

Looking back, I was shocked at how accepting they were. Even though they were worried about how I was going to manage, I was able to get off the phone with enough energy to move forward with my day. I went through a meditation and got back into a peak state which seemed to come easily. Feeling balanced in body and mind, I went to my computer and began crafting my farewell email.

What does someone say when they announce their departure? I wasn't sure, but as I started writing, the words flowed easily. The more I typed, the more sure I was about the decision. My emotions rose with each sentence I typed, and I felt my heart pouring out onto the page. I found myself crying then I was suddenly overcome with a powerful feeling of peace; everything made perfect sense. Even though it was a very big leap of faith for me, I felt like there was some divine influence in all of this. Even though I didn't know what the future would bring, I knew that somehow it was all going to work out.

I expressed gratitude in my email to everyone who had helped me, and shared the regret I felt for those who I would be leaving with a messy pile of work to clean up. I tried to explain my decision from the heart. I worked on the email until

The Departure

I felt the message was just right. I finished around 9:00 AM, just in time for everyone to be arriving at the office. As I clicked send, I was overcome with emotion. It felt like all the cells in my body were ready to burst. I had a feeling like I was in communion with a beautiful existence outside the normal, physical realm I was accustomed to. The communication from that place seemed to say clearly, "This is the right thing to do."

I closed my laptop and turned my phone on airplane mode so I could bask in this experience undisturbed. I wanted to document this feeling so I grabbed my journal and sat on the bench outside in the yard next to my cottage.

As I began writing, the feeling continued to intensify. I felt as light as a feather again, similar to my experience at the meditation gardens. It felt like the highest of highs on ecstasy but 20 times more powerful; just pure, unadulterated bliss. The words I wrote were intense, but definitely reflected how I was feeling.

Looking back on those words a few days later I was shocked, wondering if I had lost my mind. I decided that yes, I probably had. I was so crazy in fact, that for the first time in my life, I felt completely sane.

1/6/15

REMEMBER. THE WAY YOU FEEL RIGHT NOW IS WORTH IT NO MATTER HOW HARD IT GETS HOW MANY ~~FAILURES~~ ROADBLOCKS YOU ENCOUNTER. HOW MANY PEOPLE DOUBT YOU. I'M SORRY I EVER DID. I LOVE YOU. THANK YOU. LIFE STARTS NOW.

"*The feeling I'm having now is more intense than the first. This is transcendence. I've figured it out. It's scary but oh so beautiful. Everything in my life has led me to this point. It was the warm up, the pregame. Game's on now. I will head into this with my absolute focus, clarity of intent, and self-discipline.*

Times will get tough. That's life. It's what you sign up for. If we don't live it, what the FUCK is the point? I thank you for this day. It is the first step to life. The leap was hard, but I'm in for the journey."

I then started writing down a song called "Getting into You" by Reliant K.

"When I've made up my mind and my heart along with that, to live not for myself but yet for somebody else. Do you, know what you are getting yourself into? I'm getting into you, because you got to me, in a way words can't describe. I'm getting into you, because it's got to be, you're essential to survive, I'm going to love you with my life"-....

I continued my journaling:

"I figured it out...Reliant K was singing about GOD. Holy SHIT. It makes so much sense now, and I'm not crazy after all LoL! This is real. This is what life is about. This is the meaning. This is gonna be fun. Dang it no one will understand me, at least people I know, close friends. I'm honored to share the message, but I'm sure some people won't understand."

Then I wrote about my appreciation for the people who had influenced me along my path. I mentioned Seth Godin, RSD Motivation, Ryan Holiday, Paulo Coehlo, Seneca, and just as I was thinking about other people to add to my list, I looked up towards the street and saw a police suburban truck pull up.

The Departure

As six officers came rushing towards my direction, I realized I was the subject of their visit. They walked through my gate into the courtyard where I was sitting. One of the officers asked me if I was the one sending emails to my company talking about some higher calling.

A resounding "Holy Shit" went off in my brain. I knew how crazy a "higher calling" must seem to them. From my end though, I didn't understand why cops were there when all I wanted was to do some good in the world.

I suddenly felt threatened, probably not unlike a witch during the time of the Salem trials. By doing something as simple as spreading love and sharing my experiences, I was viewed with suspicion. I felt cornered, like they didn't understand where I was coming from, and that someone might think I should be locked up. I could hardly find words to explain to them what was truly going on.

They were probably thinking "you don't just quit your job for a 'higher calling'; are you crazy? Stay where you belong!" I wondered how their logic could make them think that someone in my happy state would want to kill themselves; they must have just thought I was crazy to do something so out of the norm.

Another officer asked if I had my ID. I told him it was inside, but they stopped me from going in because "there may be weapons in there!" Huhhhh? They *really* didn't understand what was going on with me. I'd really gone so sane, they thought I was insane.

One of them asked me if he could enter my home. I told him he had no right to, as I hadn't done anything wrong. I explained I had just quit my job, and told him people do that every day. One officer rebutted with "Not in the way you did."

I explained to all of them I just wanted to share my message, to travel, and help people. I told them I'd never felt so good about life. They finally got back in their vehicle and left.

With Love

Below is the email I wrote that caused someone in my company to call the police. My subject line was "With Love", because, well, that's what I wrote it with. I wrote it with the most Love I'd ever felt, and I wasn't ashamed to say so. After looking at the email again I could see where it got co-workers worried. If you worked at a corporation, what would your response be to receiving this email 9:00 AM on a Tuesday morning? (Names are substituted for privacy).

"The two most important days in your life are the day you were born and the day you find out why." -Mark Twain

The latter has come for me, and it has unfortunately come at the most inopportune time. This is the hardest, but most necessary decision I've ever had to make in my life. I truly believe we were all put here for a real reason. I've gotten the call up to the Major Leagues. I have to go play the game now, or I may never get another shot.

I feel immensely for John and all those who will feel the direct consequences of my decision to leave the company immediately. Chris, Devon, Matthew- I've left a note for you under my keyboard. Once the dust settles, I hope one day you will understand.

The Departure

I cherish the time I spent here, and the relationships I built. I hope I've inspired some of you along the way. Continue pushing the boundaries of life. It's amazing the places you'll go.

My plan is to continue to inspire and do work that matters. To help those that need it. To truly make a difference in this world. Forgive me, but I have to start right now. I pray for your support, but understand for some this is tough to hear.

Thank you Dominick for being the best boss anyone could ask for, and an even better person. You allowed me the space and encouragement to grow as an individual. That is the golden trait any manager can possess.

Thank you Rachel for being such a genuine, wholehearted individual. The unexpected nice things you would do for me meant the world. Anyone who knows you should feel lucky. I know you have so much more to give to the world, and I'm excited to see what that is.

Most importantly to Freddy:

You told me at the Christmas party I was an inspiration to you. You have no idea how much that meant to me. I have something to tell you though my friend...

YOU are the inspiration. I'll never forget you sharing your life story on how you left your parents in Mexico and came here as a teenager wanting more out of life. I can't even fathom how scared you must have been. It makes my (an upper middle class white kid with the support of his parents if he needs it) decision to embark on this journey laughable.

Find Your Truth

YOU are an inspiration to me as a Father. I can't begin to know what it's like to have a child at such a young age, and then having to raise that child on your own. You make me realize what love and family really mean. The description of your family parties describes the kind of love we all search to have, but rarely do. I hope one day I can give half as much love to my family as you give to yours.

YOU are an inspiration Freddy. Continue to want more out of life. It's short and no one is promised tomorrow. Continue learning, and never stop growing. NEVER settle. You are destined to do something great, just keep poking the box. I'm honored to call you a friend. Thank you.

I'll leave the rest of you with this...

I believe true happiness comes from becoming the person you were meant to be. You may not always be the perfect person (God knows I'm sure not) but we all have in our mind a vision of who that person is. I ask that you reflect on who that super hero is deep inside. Once you have the slightest clue of it, take some action toward becoming that person every day, however little it may be. It won't be easy, but it will be worth it.

BE THE CHANGE YOU WANT TO SEE IN THE WORLD.

With Love,
Lou
PS. I'm not suggesting you quit your job just yet. When the time comes, you'll just know. ;)

The Departure

After the police left, I went back inside to tell people I was alright. I had a few messages from co-workers who sounded like they were trying to talk me off a bridge. They had taken it seriously, and I guess I couldn't blame them. I called my ex-roommate and close friend who worked there to let him know everything was okay. I hoped that would help put out the fire I had apparently started.

I noticed I had a bunch of messages from Kelly. Although I came close to texting her that I was going to quit my job, I hadn't gone through with it so when someone passed the news along to her, it was as out of the blue for her just like it was for everyone else. Her messages startled me so I gave her a call.

She answered the phone crying, asking me if everything was alright. Apparently she was scared by the messages sent to her by one of my co-workers. Kelly then mentioned that she was at the airport during a layover on her way back to San Diego when she had heard the news about the email I had sent. She broke down, thinking she might have lost me.

She expressed relief at hearing my voice, and I was comforted to hear hers too. The police showing up had rattled me: it made me think for a moment that I *had* really gone crazy. I didn't know police protocol for someone they thought could be a suicide risk: were they supposed to hang out surveying my property, making sure I didn't do anything extreme?

The instant connection with Kelly got me out of those thoughts, if only for a moment. I had no idea that she would be flying back to San Diego that day. I asked her if it would be alright if I picked her up from the airport, and she happily agreed. She said she felt grateful that I was okay, and wanted to see me after the scare of this morning.

I got off the phone excited to be seeing her soon, but I still wanted to sit alone for awhile and process everything that had happened. My last journal entry of the day was:

"Oh man, people think I really lost it. I can't blame them. Cops actually just came a little while ago. People were concerned I was going to kill myself, when it's actually the exact opposite. I wrote that email with so much love. I was intense."

CHAPTER 38

The Truth

"I will serve as a reminder if you jump you will not fall."
— Nahko Bear

As the day went on, I felt like I was on a roller coaster of ups and downs. I took a shower to try and calm myself but it didn't help. I was having a difficult time wrapping my head around these recent events; they just weren't from this dimension. I wondered with this huge paradigm shift in my life, if I'd ever be able to function "normally" in society again. I felt like I was in this world, but that I'd been shown a richer, more meaningful place in it; for lack of better words, a higher plane of existence.

After showering and eating some breakfast, I went outside my apartment to try to clear my head and ease my fears. That was a mistake. My mind was on such high alert in a type of nervous state that I was filtering everything with a negative perspective. As I walked out of the house, I was certain the gardeners watering the plants were really just people sent by the police to make sure I wasn't going to do anything rash.

Find Your Truth

I then walked down the street to a park. I'd never been there during a weekday, and discovered it was a hub for homeless people during that time of day. I didn't have anything against homeless people, but in my current situation it wasn't the best scene to get into if drugs were involved. I'd been ecstasy-free for seven months, but the way I was feeling now reminded me of the dark side of drug use, including the paranoia. I was experiencing it in a way that made me think everyone I encountered was judging or talking about me.

I walked past the park as quickly as I could until I spotted a mailman sitting in his car eating lunch. I was sure he was working with the police too. As a matter of fact, I thought it *was* the police. I felt suspicious of everyone I passed, thinking they had been sent to watch me. Scenes from the book *1984* popped in my mind, and I felt like my community had become part of a much bigger conspiracy. It was as if everyone was partnered with the police, watching over everything at all times. My worry led me down a twisted tunnel of fear and anxiety.

I quickly realized that going outside was a bad move. I rushed back to my apartment to hide from the stress, but it was no use. It was then I remembered what I had committed to do later that afternoon; I was supposed to pick Kelly up from the airport. The airport?! How could I go to the airport in this state of mind? Scenes from the TV show "24" popped into my head where I was the terrorist being carefully watched by helicopters swirling above.

If the cops were watching me, they would certainly know I was driving to the airport. What would they think? "He was a possible suicide threat and now he's driving to the airport; maybe he's planning some kind of attack." This is just one example of the many types of ideas running through my mind. They all seemed like very real possibilities from my perspective; I was definitely in my own world.

The Truth

I learned from this experience that in some cases there is really no such thing as fear. Most stressful situations we find ourselves in are often just our *perception* of reality; scary situations can be completely self-created just because of the filters we use to interpret what's going on around us. I was getting a crash course in how we all invent stories in our minds that in turn have a huge impact on the way we view the world. The story I was telling myself was that I was being monitored by the government. Each encounter I had with people was perceived and understood through that filter. I felt so scared at one point that I even considered sending an Uber to pick Kelly up from the airport so I wouldn't have to go outside. My fear was causing me to want to hide in retreat.

You might be asking, if his mind was inventing such stories, maybe the experiences during the five-day spiritual journey were all in his imagination too? My response is simple: my personal journey was about getting out of my own way and letting Love guide me. When you do that, there's no experience like it, and it's different for everyone. I *had* let love guide me, but then fear started creeping in.

These fears reminded me of a scene in Napoleon Hill's *Outwitting the Devil*. Napoleon was hiding out in a basement for a year, paralyzed by fear, doubt, worry, and limitations. He finally snapped out of this depression after finding his "other self." He realized that all his fears had been "made up" in his mind. He found the courage and faith to leave, to pursue his ultimate purpose. He shared these insights and personal growth in his writings, and I'm grateful I read about them. Because I was able to learn from his experiences, I suffered only a few hours of paralyzing fear, rather than a year or longer.

The time came to leave for the airport and I still had the irrational, anxiety-laden feeling of being watched. I believed that driving to the airport might result in a bombardment of special forces aimed specifically at taking me down. Even though I felt this fear, I realized that if I didn't pick Kelly up, I would be losing much more.

So it was with extreme trepidation that I walked out to my car. As I opened the door, one guiding phrase gave me strength: "I'm going to pick up my woman."

Driving to the airport was one of the most unnerving experiences of my life, and it was all due to the paranoia-based story playing out in my mind. Every car that got behind me seemed like they were following me, talking on their phones walkie-talkie style. While they were probably just talking to friends, what I saw was a team of undercover police keeping tabs on me. What I heard in my imagination was, "We got him, heading south on Hawthorne, seems like he's headed to the airport!"

As one car turned a different direction another car got behind, taking its place. By what seemed to be no coincidence to me at the time, this next person was holding his phone to his ear and staring directly at me, which I could see through my rearview mirror. My heart was pounding. I imagined various scenes which could play out when I got to the airport.

I felt like when I hit the terminal road that I would be bombarded with police officers from every direction, sirens blaring and guns drawn. I honestly thought that it might happen, but that wasn't going to stop me from my mission to pick up Kelly. "I'm going to pick up my woman. Even if I they start firing and I get shot, so be it", I told myself.

I called Kelly as I pulled up to the terminal. The phone rang twice then the call disconnected. I immediately thought: "They must have got to her!" Maybe the cops thought she was in this with me. I called her again. No answer. I continued to panic until I saw her.

The Truth

I pulled up and she quickly threw her bags in the back seat and jumped into the car. As her car door closed, so did all my concerns. All the paranoia and fear I had built up in my mind washed away like sand from the ocean waves. As we embraced, I felt surrounded by love. It was as if I had been in a cool shaded place and suddenly the sun burst through with its warming rays. I felt comforted, and my mind was finally at peace.

We didn't say a word to each other. We couldn't because both of us were crying. As I pulled away from her, the past five awe-inspiring days of new awareness hit me like a ton of bricks. Everything that had happened had led up to this moment: the hike, the gardens, the realizations, the leap of faith... Everything led me back to my angel, my one true love.

As this realization dawned, a new wave of emotion came over me. I decided then that I wanted to go to a beautiful location in San Diego called Sunset Cliffs. Through the onslaught of tears and love, another epiphany came to me: the perfectness of the situation was profound. The love I was feeling was the deepest it had been through all of my recent "spiritual" experiences, and I realized if there was ever a good time to propose to the woman I loved, it was then.

I didn't have a ring and I didn't have a plan, but I knew this love needed to be expressed. I pulled up to the cliffs and invited Kelly to get out of the car with me. She did and we embraced in a big hug. Then, with the most love I'd ever felt, I dropped down to one knee.

I told Kelly how I felt, pouring out every last bit of my heart. I wish I had recorded it because trying to put that whole experience into words would be impossible. I told her how I'd be there to support us and our future children and how I'd show our family the deepest love imaginable. I told her I wanted to spend my whole life sharing everything that had happened over the past week and what I'd experienced, and I prayed that she would trust me. When I finished sharing my feelings of love and appreciation, I asked her to marry me.

A few long seconds passed before she answered. During that pause, there was a moment where I feared she might say no. It was a moment of dismay for me until through her tears and sobs, she said yes.

I'm not sure where I'd be right now if she had said no; honestly I don't want to think about it. In my time of uncertainty, my angel had come to guide me. It was as if I was experiencing heaven on earth; the pinnacle to an amazing, crazy five days had come. The time we spent together during the next few hours was the most blissful time of my life.

As the sun set, we danced around like we were at an EDM music festival, except no music was playing and the drug we were on was the best life had to offer. I was in complete and utter bliss. I felt that all that had happened was an amazing set of experiences, all leading me to this time of Kelly and I being together again. With every part of my being I knew I had reached a level of awareness through all this, and it had become clear that Kelly was my "soulmate". I could hardly believe how things had unfolded so completely.

We lay down to watch the sun's rays gleam off the ocean. It was a picturesque January evening and everything felt perfect. I felt like I had just taken the ride of my life, and this was the best part. I was reaping the rewards of taking such a big leap of faith into the unknown. Then I realized how cinematic the past five days had been, and I got up and yelled out to the open sky: "THIS IS A FUCKING MOVIE! I'M GOING TO MAKE A MOVIE!!"

The people nearby who had been trying to enjoy a relaxing sunset were surely wondering who this crazy person was screaming and dancing at the top of his lungs. It's not that I

The Truth

didn't care; I just honestly didn't even notice anyone there besides Kelly and me. It was as if we were on our own private paradise, basking in a special cocktail of bliss that only occurs when soulmates unite in such a magical fusion.

I wanted that moment to last forever. I wanted to bask in that amazing feeling because when you tap into and experience something so divine, nothing else can come close to it. However, the sun was setting and it was time for us to head home so I drove her back to my apartment, unable to really process all that had happened that day.

In one day I had quit my job, got questioned for suspicion of suicide, fought extreme paranoia, then proposed to the woman I love. It was safe to say I hadn't had a day quite like that in my life before, and likely wouldn't again.

It was a pivotal time in my life; it was the end of the person I was with no bridge or life boat to get back. I had hurled myself into the unknown with nothing but hope and a prayer. I was shown the immense power and awe of the universe as it brought me and my soulmate back together. I couldn't waste a minute of it, so I acted on the love I felt.

That day will always be remembered and held in the deepest place of my heart. It was the start of a brand new life, away from the reality I had known that had suddenly become an illusion. It was my journey while in the hands of a higher intelligence. I wasn't sure why it had all happened, but it was clear to me that the future was a wonderful destiny. I had followed the call, and I was ready; well, as ready as a person could be when they have no idea what they're doing or what lies ahead. For me, those were big questions.

What was I going to do with this brand new life?

The Conclusion

There isn't a day that goes by that I'm not grateful for the decision I made to quit my job. For a 25-year-old who'd been comfortably on one path my whole life, leaving everything I knew was the scariest thing I'd ever done. I've been blessed with the support from Kelly in this brand new life, but I still had to navigate through the uncertainty.

My purpose in writing this book was to share some of the experiences of my journey to find the truth; *my* truth. During this discovery process I experienced what some people call a Higher Power, God, the Universe, Spirit, or a Connection to all things. I also found a purpose to life, and comfort in knowing that I was (and am) guided by forces hardly imaginable to the human mind. Until I had these personal experiences I had never known such a world even existed, despite the fact that I had been raised in a church-going family. It was my connection to this power that gave me strength through the ups and downs that came with making such a drastic change.

I understand some readers may not believe in God, a higher power or whatever they want to call it. That's fine; you don't have to believe. I didn't. If that's the case for you, let this book be an example of how shifting your actions and perspective can lead to a more "naturally" engaged and happy life. You don't need drugs to do it. If you're someone who searches for happiness, peace or excitement in a pill or powder, you should know that bliss is really out there and that it can be found in other ways.

My experiences made me want to share with others what a purposeful and genuinely happy life can be like. I wanted to help others understand my personal journey and also offer a practical guide with steps that lead to what some refer to as a connection to "spirit". This is my ultimate goal; to inspire others to find their truth, their purpose, their bliss. I'm so grateful I experienced this paradigm shift and got an introductory crash course on the art of living with purpose.

If you think you can't change the circumstances in your life, I hope this book shows you that at any moment, you can. You always have a choice about every aspect of your life. If you deny that choice, you deny your freedom. Personal development and living your passion takes work. You have to fight your inner demons which might have been ignored for a long time, shed light on them and go through some challenges. It may be scary to face the fears that come up but that's part of the work.

After I quit my job, many of my close friends and family thought I was crazy. This book was originally planned to try to help them understand what was going on with me. It's nearly impossible to relate to such a profound and personally meaningful experience from an intellectual point of view. It's also just as difficult to try to explain it in a way people can understand. I'm sure I'll be figuring that out my entire life, but regardless, it's been very rewarding to support others on their journey. Through this process, I've developed a real desire to help guide others to (or through) their own personal transformation.

The Conclusion

I've come to accept that it might be hard to understand. I'm actually happy about it, because I know this is my story and no one else's. Everyone has their own journey, a sacred experience that is uniquely personal, something between themselves and their creator.

At the time all this happened I didn't really understand what was going on. I didn't know about the ins and outs of something often referred to as a "spiritual awakening"; let alone spirituality in general. My learning about it actually came by experience. With no "big picture" understanding of these experiences and what it all meant, the months that followed after I quit my job brought some confusing highs and lows. I came to realize over time that everything was unfolding in what can only be described as destiny, perfect timing, or divine order.

If I had known then what I know now, I might have been able to avoid some of the struggles. It's my hope that this book finds its way to someone who might have gone, or is going through similar experiences. It can be a very lonely place, and a little understanding goes a long way. If you're reading this and you feel like I'm talking directly to you, please reach out. In the meantime know that there is only *Love*. Any fear you're feeling is part of your growth process, to help you become the person you're destined to be.

That's how I'm living my life now, as the person I was meant to be. I want to guide people to find their destiny too. I want to inspire others to use the life they were given to create whatever masterpiece they know is calling to them. If you asked me what I do today, I'd say that first and foremost, I inspire. The medium sometimes changes, but in general that's what I feel called to do. I want to inspire you so YOU can do what inspires you.

Find Your Truth

This is my purpose; it's what fills me with life. Being selfless is actually the most selfish thing I can do. If I can inspire more people to live a life they love, then I'm in great company. If I can inspire YOU to do things that excite you the most, then you're a happier person to be around. You have a positive impact on people you encounter on a day to day basis, and they see you and say, "I need some of that in my life." They might ask questions and possibly go on their own personal journey. At that point you've become the inspiration, and the domino effect goes on and on. I'm just a pawn making my move in the game of life: I hope you choose to play it, too.

Share a similar goal with me by making your life your message. Take bold action as often as possible and you'll go far. It's my hope that I can lead with that boldness. Since I began my involvement with World Travelers Association, I've been on travel retreats around the world that focus on adventure and volunteering. I look forward to seeing the impact these activities make on the world in future years.

I surround myself with people like Jorge at World Travelers Association now: people who live an inspired life and enjoy all that life has to offer. Take some time to look at people around you: are their thoughts, words or actions supportive and encouraging? Do you feel good or bad when you're around them? Are they living the type of life you want to lead? Living a purposeful life also involves conscious choices about who's in yours.

Thank you so much for picking up this book and joining me on my journey to find truth. While it seems like I "found" my truth, more descriptive words could be "shown" or "revealed". The truth is within all of us and we each have our own path to it; our own unique Truth. Don't ever be afraid to speak your truth when the time is right for you because for every person

The Conclusion

who does, there are dozens more who need to hear it and follow their example. Truth resonates. Truth heals.

That said, I'll end in the way I left my corporate job on that faithful day:

With Love.

How I can Support You

I decided to write this book just one month after quitting my job; I posted on Facebook that I'd have it completed in 90 days. It was an ambitious goal, but it gave me the social pressure to keep writing, even when I doubted myself. The truth is, it took me two years to finish and publish it. Here's what I learned: when working on something you feel called to do, you will doubt yourself. You will think you're no good. You will question why you started and think about giving up.

If it wasn't for the people I looked towards for guidance I might have let my limiting beliefs win and you wouldn't be reading this. The past two years I've been supported every step of the way to make this dream a reality. It's now my mission to support you on your journey. I want to make your dream a reality. Let me know how I can by reaching out through my website, Louredmond.com.

See you there.

Made in United States
Orlando, FL
12 September 2023